POSITIONED
2
PROSPER

Eight Golden Nuggets to Ensure Your Prosperity

For Women By Women

By

NADIA M. HARRIS

Failure is never final, it is simply a part of the process on the journey.

Where powerful people in prominent places pour into your purpose

www.Positione2dProsper.com

DISCLAIMER

Information presented within this book represents the sole view of the authors and publisher and is intended for informational purposes only, as of the date of publication. This book offers no private or professional advice. The reader is encouraged to use good judgment when applying the information herein contained and to seek advice from a qualified professional, if needed.

The authors and publisher shall, in no event be held liable for any loss or other damaged, including but not limited to special, incidental, consequential, or other damages. All references for any subjective decision made as to their content and//or use.

Positioned 2 Prosper Publishing

Positioned2ProsperBooks@gmail.com

www.Positioned2Prosper.com

DEDICATION

This book is dedicated to all the beautiful women desiring a transformation in their lives. The single mothers working day and night to provide for their children. The wives who understand that being and wife is the first ministry to our husbands. That CEO who has to deal with the challenges of running a business and still has to demand the respect as their male counterparts. That teenage mother who feels like her dreams and goals now have to be pushed aside and she can never become that College Graduate, Doctor, Lawyer, Educator, Engineer, Etc., that she always dreamed of becoming. I dedicate this book to the grandmothers that never lost hope and continued to stand in the gap for the children, always praying and believing God for a miracle. The grandmother that always had a smile, encouraging word and that much needed hug to give to whomever needed it at that moment. This book is dedicate to the many mentors and mentees who give of their time, energy and effort to make a difference in so many lives.

Thank you, from your sister-friends. It is a pleasure and honor to serve you with the knowledge and wisdom that has transformed our lives.

In His Service,

ACKNOWLEDGMENTS

I humbly thank my Lord for without Him and His grace, none of this would be possible. I want to especially thank Apostle Dr. Bethtina Williams, Pastor Tara L. Alexander, Bridgette R. Smith, Brenda Stroman, Sheryl King, Joyce C. Stewart, Evangelist Patsy Cole, Dr. Jacqueline Mohair and Evangelist Chante A. Kelly for sharing with the world the wisdom and knowledge gained through life lessons. Each one of you are jewels and such a great Blessing to me and so many others. Your transparency and desire to reach the masses with your message is priceless. Thank you!

Nadia M. Harris

To Our Kings

Thank you to our Kings – Husbands, Fathers, Grand Fathers, Brothers, Uncles, Sons, Pastors, Etc., who cover, protect and, provide for us and lead selflessly. We honor and appreciate you.

Why you should read

<u>Positioned 2 Prosper</u>

Eight Golden Nuggets To Ensure Your Prosperity

Positioned 2 Prosper will cause a disruption in your negative thought process or what you may have thought to be prosperity. Each chapter is designed to catapult your thinking to a place where true prosperity awaits. Prospering in every area of your life is the manifestation of what God desires for all. The mind, will, emotion, intellect and imagination are just a few areas that most women may not recognize as part of the soul that should prosper as well. As you prepare for this journey with your sister friends just know that we are real women with real issues that have sought out real solutions that work and if you dare to join this journey and work consistently and on purpose you to will become Positioned 2 Prosper.

Nadia M. Harris

Remembering Our Sister Friend Brenda Stroman

Brenda Stroman a Phenomenal Woman

This world was blessed to have you, so many lives where touched, transformed, educated, empowered and inspired by your presence. I've said to you how grateful I am that you took time out of your busy life to edit my work. You never said no even though you had tons of obligations.

When I asked you in 2015 to be a part of my book project again you so graciously accepted and thanks to you and my other sister friends this book Positioned 2Prosper has blessed and will continue to bless so many lives. On behalf of the co-authors, your sister friends of Positioned 2Prosper Book for Women By Women. Thank you for your servant's heart. You will be missed by many but never forgotten.

Rest in Peace

Table of Contents

CHAPTER ONE

❧

Spiritually Wealthy

Apostle Dr. Bethtina Williams

A Spiritually Wealthy Woman

Wealth is a term that encompasses the condition of being happy, prosperous and of spiritual well-being. Wealth begins in the heart and mind of a person, just as poverty begins in the heart and mind of a person. How you are doing and fairing on the inside has as much to do with how you are doing and fairing on the outside as developing healthy eating habits are to ensure that you live a vibrant lifestyle. It all is a part of the way a person thinks oftentimes in spite of the difficulties and challenges they face. For example, Mother

Teresa of Calcutta, India lived in the midst of some of the most improvised conditions as she assisted countless numbers of souls with some of the most basic necessities of life. Yet, she had a wealthy spirit and raised awareness concerning the need to help our fellow man and those who are in impoverished conditions around the world. As a result of her work, Mother Teresa has gone down in history as one of the world's greatest humanitarians. Hence, being a spiritually wealthy woman has everything to do with a person's heart and mindset. A wealthy heart begins with how you see yourself and others around you. In the book of 3 John 1:2, the Apostle John states, *"Beloved, I wish above all things that thou mayest prosper and be in health, even as thy soul prospereth."* Here, the Apostle John is speaking to Gauis, whom he esteemed highly and held dear, letting him know that his greatest desire was to see him have a prosperous and successful journey in life, and be in good health even as his soul, psuche in the Greek language encompassing the heart, mind, and seat of one's inner feelings, desires, and affections, "prospereth."

Prosperity and wealth go hand in hand. They are derivatives of the collective internal core values, wisdom, priorities, principles, and spiritual well-being that a person possesses. Prosperity is defined by

Baker's Evangelical Dictionary of Bible Theology as wealth. They are interchangeable in terms of possessing a wealthy or prosperous mindset in which the core values and inner principles which govern a person's belief system are strong, effective and are of a high standard. In reality wealth and prosperity encompass much more than mere material things, although material riches should be considered as a very important aspect of what it means to be prosperous and wealthy. A wealthy person is someone who is able to successfully transfer, communicate and instill their most valued beliefs, principles, and successes to others, especially to the next generation. It's even better when tangible riches and finances accompany the process. However, tangible riches and finances alone do not constitute what it means to be wealthy. In the strongest sense, wealth is holistic encompassing the entire perspective of the total well-being of a person spiritually, mentally, emotionally, relationally, physically, and financially.

There are many examples of people who have great accumulation of material things and money, whose health is failing. Those people would give any amount of money to recover their health, but money alone cannot bring physical healing. Having a healthy strong relationship with God can bring hope, healing and restoration not only physically, but in every area of life. So, in essence it can be said that true wealth, which again is holistic in nature, begins with one's relationship with Jesus Christ.

As women of God we need to understand and know that wealth is a part of God's original intent from the beginning of time. It was all inclusive, meaning that everything man needed was bountifully provided in the Garden of Eden. Adam and Eve had it all – optimum health, relationship with God, every resource known to man and also dominion. According to Genesis 1:26, *"And God said, Let us make man in our image, after our likeness: and let them have dominion over the fish of the sea, and over the fowl of the air, and over the cattle, and over all the earth, and over every creeping thing that creepeth upon the earth."* (NIV) Dominion represents sovereignty, control, authority, mastery, power and rule over a territory, possession or government. God wants to put you back into the driver's seat so that you are not living at the mercy of whatever things dictate to you from the outside in, but you can acknowledge

God in all of your ways and He will guide you into a victorious way of living as the head and not the tail, above only and not beneath. As you acknowledge God, He will give you the grace, strength and power to take control of your life and walk in dominion authority which is His original intent from the beginning with Adam and Eve. In fact the word dominion is a term that can be described as a kingdom principle. Matthew 6:33 says, *"But seek ye first the kingdom of God, and his righteousness; and all these things shall be added unto you."* (KJV) Rather than seeking and being in pursuit of a career or material things first, the Scripture instructs us to prioritize our pursuit after the "kingdom of God, and His righteousness" first as the primary most important and highest ranking objective in life.

The kingdom of God, basileia *{bas-il-i'-ah}* in the Greek language, represents royal power, kingship, dominion, rule; the authority to rule over a kingdom or territory. Therefore, it can be clearly delineated and seen that God is a king who rules over all things. Psalm 24:1, "*The earth is the Lord's, and the fullness thereof; the world, and they that dwell therein.*" (KJV) As we honor God and reverence of His authority, power and rule, we are also to include the pursuit of His righteousness which is described by the Greek word *dikaiosune {dik-ah-yos-oo'-nay}*, the right way of being, thinking, and doing things that is acceptable to God. It pertains to having integrity, virtue, purity of life, rightness, correctness of thinking, feeling, and acting which represents the kingdom of God. At the very heart of the issue is the fact that true wealth begins with one's relationship with God and the content of one's character, then "*all these things will be added unto thee*" according to Matthew 6:33. What "things" are the Scripture speaking of? Things is defined as "*these words,*" *tauta {tow'-tah}* in the Greek language, and pertains

to the words and promises of God. This is amazing because what it denotes is an immeasurable supply of anything and everything that pertains unto life and godliness, and has no limitations!

When you seek first the kingdom of God as the primary most important thing, and pursue His manner of doing things, acting, believing and speaking, God's unlimited supply of kingdom resources is made available to you. It is placed at your disposal so that everything you need is bountifully supplied with nothing missing, nothing lacking and nothing broken. The key is found in seeking the kingdom of God, not mere religion as a formality that is stepped in tradition and hinders people from experiencing the very best that God ordained for them. The Bibles tells us that the traditions of men make the word of God of none effect. (Mathew 15:6; Mark 7:13)

If you desire to experience the highest degree of wealthy living that is free from dead religion, and is full of the Spirit, life, power and word of God acknowledge Him first as the highest and most important priority. I have experienced some of the greatest joys in life through my relationship with Jesus Christ. I have traveled all over the world and lived in different countries in which I have had some priceless experiences such as, seeing lives transformed, healed, restored and delivered by the authority of God's word and the power of His promise.

I have witnessed the fruits of being a spiritually wealthy and prosperous woman firsthand through the power of prayer and meditation upon the Word of God. The rich fulfillment that comes from having a rich meaningful relationship with God is beyond measure. It yields great results. I have personally watched God manifest himself thousands of times in my own life as well as in the lives of those who I have ministered to over the years. The most profound thing I have noticed over all is how God responds to a need, not based on how great or small it is, but by the faith and agreement that is released from the hearts of the individuals who are seeking God in prayer. Notably, many people have called me to pray for them for many years, and I have literally felt the power of God be released from my spirit when the connection of agreement and faith was made with mine by the person asking for prayer. You see, when faith and agreement exist between any number of people who are seeking God in prayer it releases the power and anointing of God into their situation, which in turn creates very prosperous results.

I love to read and study the word of God, because it contains the promises of God, and faith-filled obedience to His word produces prosperity according to the book of Joshua 1:8. It says, "This book of the law shall not depart out of thy mouth; but thou shalt meditate therein day and night, that thou mayest observe to do according to all that is written therein: for then thou shalt make thy way prosperous, and then thou shalt have good success." Therefore, if we keep the precepts of God's word on the forefront of our hearts and meditate upon his promise which means to mutter, speak, think on what God has spoken both day and night and implement it, then we will "*make our way prosperous and have good success.*" In other words, God has given to us the capacity to initiate actions that will result in obtaining a way, journey or manner of life that is successful, progressive, advancing and prosperous. You will literally break out of what is happening to you that is beneath the privilege of the promises of God and enter into a remarkably better way of life that is filled with measurable progress, good success, and advancement.

A spiritually wealthy woman is prosperous, because she knows how to walk by faith calling those things which are not as though they already do exist. (Romans 4:17) She understands that the promises of God's word have the power to bring manifestation. It is from the wealth of God's word that is stored up in her heart that she prays and obtains great results. Faith and prayer are major characteristics of a spiritually wealthy woman. Additionally, a spiritually wealthy and prosperous woman is wise-hearted, virtuous, integral, resourceful, insightful, productive, a good planner, she organizes well, prepares, sees things through to the finish, achieves her personal goals, builds a lasting legacy and heritage of faith for her family and others, takes time for herself, gives quality time to her family, shares of her substance with others in need, has a good heart, uplifts and esteems others and never devalues them, she loves to help others excel and advance, raises the standard and holds herself accountable to it, exercises discipline and godly judgment, is focused, examines her own strengths and weaknesses, promises small but delivers big, underwrites projects, makes a positive contribution to meaningful projects, excels beyond the norm, is a visionary leader, intelligent thinker, uses her creative abilities to enhance every endeavor she is committed to. A spiritually wealthy woman is a difference maker! Everything she does is made better and improved because of her presence.

A prosperous and wealthy woman knows who she is, and knows the true and living God. She is comfortable in her own skin, and is secure with her identity. She knows very well that she is *"fearfully and wonderfully made"* according to Psalm 139:14. When you have this type of mindset and understanding about who you are, no limits or boundaries can restrict you from excelling into the highest degree of success in life. Nothing can stop your progress, success, or drive to reach your goals. I have had the distinguished privilege of working with some of the most successful women in America, and without exception each one possesses a keen awareness of who they are, why they are here and what their purpose is. In addition, they are willing to share with others out of the abundance of wealth God has graced them with. Wealth is more than being born with a silver spoon in your mouth. It is an experience born out of a strong awareness that God's word is true. He has given you all things that pertain unto life and godliness, and you can have everything that God's word promises to you.

Throughout the course of my life, I have given myself to live by the principles and promises of God's word which has resulted in taking me to places I only dreamed of before. It has allowed me the honor of building strong relationships with some of the greatest people in the world, and be able to contribute synergistically and mutually to their lives. I have been mightily blessed by God to marry the most faithful, integral, caring, loving, and godly man whose support has encouraged me to accomplish my goals and destiny in life. Giving birth to and raising our sons together has to be the most rewarding experience and success of my life beyond everything else. I truly believe that I have learned more in the process of instilling godly principles and values in them as they have grown and matured into young men than all of the college degrees, education, professional certifications and accomplishments I have made combined. In my opinion, the most important thing to remember as you seek God and reach to acquire greater dimensions of success and prosperity in life is to remember that you cannot do it without the awareness that God is your ultimate source, and he sovereignly uses people as his special agents in the earth to help you to succeed. Always stay humble, thankful, and share out of the wealth you have been blessed to have with others. In doing so, you become a conduit and vessel who brings glory, honor and praise to God. My earnest prayer is to see you excel, live the life of your dreams, and fulfill your purpose and destiny. You can do it if you believe in yourself and have a deep sense of abiding faith in the God who created you. He wired you, fashioned and formed you for good success.

Bio of Apostle,

Dr. Bethtina Q. Williams

Her Excellency, Apostle Dr. Bethtina Williams is the Founder of MPowering Lives International, Inc., and Co-Founder of Lighthouse of Faith Community Church. She is a published author of the book entitled "Women of Character & Destiny", which is distributed worldwide. She is a Professionally Certified Executive Life Coach and Empowerment Specialist, internationally recognized General in Prayer, Anointed Psalmist, Certified Chaplain and Ambassador at Large to the UN, and Humanitarian who has traveled nationally and internationally for over 30 years fulfilling her passion of ministering to women and men alike helping them to breakthrough every limitation and barrier, to maximize their potential and fulfill their destiny. She is happily married to Apostle, Dr. Stanley Williams, Sr. for 30 years. Together they have three handsome sons, Stanley II, Jonathan, and Joshua.

Her Excellency, Dr. Bethtina Williams was consecrated into the Apostolic Office by her Covering and Mentor HRM, King Adamtey I (King of the Se State of Ghana, West Africa & known in private life as Dr. Kingsley Fletcher), Bishop Anthony J. Hatcher and Apostle, Dr. Larry Carnes on March 16, 2012. The Honorable Mike Anderson,

Mayor of the City of Fort Walton Beach, FL declared March 16, 2012 to be Dr. Bethtina Williams and Dr. Stanley Williams Day in the History of the City. She has trained and ministered to leaders in the body of Christ extensively throughout the United States, Europe and Africa for many years, and has served to help establish ministries and churches in the United States to which she also serves as an apostolic covering in the Lord.

Apostle Dr. Bethtina Williams is also a member of Life Community Fellowship of Pastors founded by HRM, King Adamtey I (known in private life as Dr. Kingsley Fletcher, king of the Se State, Ghana, West Africa). He is her mentor, spiritual covering and father in the faith. She is also a protégé of Dr. N. Cindy Trimm, a 21st Century World Leader, empowerment specialist, and best-selling author. Dr. Williams attended Texas Tech University for her undergraduate studies, and is a distinguished Alumni of FI Christian University with a Bachelor's Degree in Administration, Master's Degree in Biblical Studies, and an earned Doctor of Ministry degree. In December 2014, Her Excellency, Dr. Williams received an Honorary Doctorate of Divinity Degree, Certified Chaplaincy, and Ambassador at Large from CICA University where the Honorable Dr. Phillip S. Phinn, OEA is the International Chairman & Chancellor. Her Chaplaincy and Ambassadorship at Large is formally recognized by the United Nations.

Apostle Bethtina Williams is the author of "Women of Character and Destiny" forwarded by Dr. Kingsley Fletcher, as a powerful book that is filled with answers and solutions for the issues women face today. It has been distributed worldwide and can be obtained at: www.MpoweringLives.com, Barnes and Noble Bookstore online, and Amazon (in paperback and Kindle version).

Apostle Dr. Bethtina Williams has been a featured guest on Trinity Broadcasting Network on numerous occasions, on The Word Network, and Manna Television in Dallas, Texas. She has also been very instrumental in producing the LIVE Streaming Internet TV program for LFCC, with a global audience, and LFCC Television Programming on "Preach the Word Worldwide Network, which has reached over 23 million people throughout the Tallahassee, FL region, across the United States and the world.

You may contact Apostle Williams for ministry invitations via email at *drbethwilliams@gmail.com* or on her ministry website at *www. MPoweringLives.com.*

CHAPTER TWO

∽

Intellect

Dr. Jacqueline Mohair

Intellectual Wealth

Intelligence *Grace* Wisdom

James 3:13

Who among you is wise and understanding? Let him show by his good behavior his deeds in the gentleness of wisdom.

What is intelligence? Intelligence is the capacity to acquire and apply knowledge. Grace is the free and unmerited favor of God, as manifested in the salvation of sinners and the bestowal of blessings. Wisdom is the accumulated knowledge that gives the ability to discern or judge what is true, right, or lasting; gives the common sense; gives insight. As we begin to look at the differences between the three terms, intelligence is normally construed to be the amount of information gathered in the human brain. Wisdom on the other hand is the intelligence that we gain in the process of learning from the mistakes that we commit. Grace is unmerited divine assistance given humans for their regeneration or sanctification, a virtue coming from God.

Intelligence on the contrary implies the cause of anything executed impeccably. If a younger person is adept in avoiding mistakes then we usually hear the famous phrase "he is wise beyond his years'. It is thus understood that wisdom is nothing but intelligence in personal experience. All you have to do in gaining wisdom is know how best not to make mistakes after committing them.

One of the main difference between intelligence and wisdom is that intelligence is the knowledge gained without making a mistake, whereas wisdom is the knowledge gained by making mistakes. However, it is through the fear of God that true wisdom is birthed. Only Grace makes alive. A shorthand for what grace is - "Mercy, not merit." Grace is the opposite of karma, which is all about getting what you deserve. Grace and Mercy shall follow me all the days of my life. Grace and Mercy is what keeps us in the midst of making decisions based only out of intellect with no wisdom. *Grace is sufficient in all our needs.* You can define wisdom in another way too. It is absolutely right to define wisdom as intelligence that is used. It would quite naturally mean that if intelligence is not properly put to use then you are not considered a man with wisdom.

If a person is considered highly intelligent but not wise enough, then it means that the person is not learning from the mistakes he has been making. His intelligence simply survives on the knowledge he gained by the few mistakes that he has not made. I can relate to this one on numerous occasions. As a child I ask the Lord to make me wise. However, I did not know that it would cost me. Yes, it cost numerous of bad decisions and not listening to the wisdom of others. My father would tell me that bought sense is better than any. Wow! Did I find out? Only when I begin the relationship with the father was when wisdom begin to open up. Thank God for his Grace and Mercy! Intellect without wisdom can be a dangerous thing. To know God is the beginning of wisdom.

Proverbs 9:10

The fear of the LORD is the beginning of wisdom, And the knowledge of the Holy One is understanding.

The bible tells us the fear of the Lord is the beginning of wisdom. Therefore, you can have intellect but without God there is no discernment. In this hour we need discernment, wisdom (mother whit) to foresee what God is saying in this hour. The word says that knowledge of the Holy One is understanding. According to the book of Job "*And to man He said, 'Behold, the fear of the Lord, that is wisdom; And to depart from evil is understanding*" The bible tells us in Psalms that the fear of the LORD is the beginning of wisdom; A good understanding has all those who do His commandments; His praise endures forever. All through the word we find out what wisdom is but how many times have we ignored the holy spirit? How many times have you made a decision based off of your head knowledge and not your gut? How many times have you made a decision and something in your spirit was not agreeing with your head knowledge? *Let mespeakfor me!* A lot of times I made decisions off of my head and not discernment and it cost me. Discernment (my gut) tells me to check it when my intellect tells me it's ok. Are you ignoring the signs when the Holy Spirit is speaking to you? We get in trouble when we are not listening to wisdom (discernment). However, through the knowledge of Christ I was able to learn and grow from impromptu decisions. A man or woman with wisdom should naturally be endowed with sufficient intelligence also. Simply because of the fact that he or she has gained a lot of knowledge by making mistakes and thereby gained intelligence in the process since he or she might have gained knowledge even by not making the same mistakes. It is important to note that wisdom cannot be taught whereas intelligence, intellect is gained when something is taught.

James 3:13

Who among you is wise and understanding? Let him show by his good behavior his deeds in the gentleness of wisdom.

The signification of wisdom, as being those things which are of the will in the internal man; from the signification of intelligence, as being those things which are of the will and of the consequent effect in the external man. Exodus thirty one verse 3 states that by *the words have I filled him with the spirit of God, in wisdom, and intelligence, and in knowledge, and in all kinds of skills.* This signifies all things of the man who is in the good of celestial love, both interior and exterior, which receive the influx of Divine truth from the Lord and from this are in enlightenment. Those that do not know what the internal and external man is and also what the understanding is and what the will, cannot apprehend in what manner wisdom, intelligence, knowledge, and work are distinct from one another for the reason that they cannot have a distinct idea of the one and of the other. Wherefore they who have not this knowledge call him or her wise who is only intelligent; nay, who merely has knowledge. But he or she is wise who does truth from love; he is intelligent who does them from faith; he has knowledge who does them from knowledge; and work denotes that which is done from all these; thus work denotes their effect in which they conjoin themselves together.

Wherefore in the genuine sense no one can be called wise, nor intelligent, nor as possessing knowledge, who does not do these things. For wisdom and intelligence and knowledge are all of life, and not of doctrine without life; for the life is the end for the sake of which these are. Such therefore as is the end, such are the wisdom, the intelligence, and the knowledge. If the end is genuine good, which is the good of love to the Lord and of charity toward the neighbor, then there are wisdom, intelligence, and knowledge in their proper sense; for then they are with the man from the Lord. But if the end is for the sake of the good of the love of self and of the world, they are not wisdom, intelligence, and knowledge, because in this case they are with the man from himself. There was a time when all I wanted what I wanted. How selfish of me to think it was all about me? For the good of the love of self and of the world as the end is evil, and of evil as the end it is by no means possible to predicate anything of wisdom and of intelligence, or even of knowledge; for what is knowledge unless there is in it the intelligence of truth and the wisdom of good, seeing that in this case it causes the man to think that what is evil is good and that what is false is true?

With those who are in the good of love to the Lord, wisdom, intelligence, knowledge, and work, follow together in order from innermost to outermost. With such men, wisdom is inmost, for it is to will well from love; intelligence is second for it is to understand well from willing well. These two are of the internal man. Knowledge consists in knowing well, and work in doing well, both from willing well. These two are of the external man. From this it is evident that wisdom must be intelligence, intelligence in knowledge, and knowledge in work. Thus work includes and brings to a conclusion all the interior things, for it is the ultimate in which they close.

According to the book of Ephesians it says that for it is by grace [God's remarkable compassion and favor drawing you to Christ] that you have been saved [actually delivered from judgment and given eternal life] through faith. And this [salvation] is not of yourselves [not through your own effort], but it is the [undeserved, gracious] gift of God; not as a result of [your] works [nor your attempts to keep the Law], so that no one will [be able to] boast or take credit in any way [for his salvation]. Therefore, we are made alive in Christ through Grace. *We can shout right there! If it had not been for the Grace of God where would we be if not in Christ!* We would be lost without Christ... to know Christ we have life ... Don't know Christ, then you are controlled by your flesh and your own intellect without wisdom.

Positioned 2 Prosper Wisdom Nugget to Ensure Your Prosperity

As we begin to look at our lives and business we need to examine our thought process. What is intellect saying about your vision? What is your gut (discernment) saying? The truth without wisdom your intellect can lead you down a maze that could have been eliminated simply by seeking God. When we start the journey seeking the Kingdom of God and only then will the other things be added to you. The enemy will throw all types of distractions your way to keep you from spending time with God. We have got to fight the good fight of faith and push forward no matter what. In order to do so we must recognize the enemy's tactics and fight back with a strategy. We must take back everything the enemy has stolen from us. *Now back to the prosperity nugget.* The word of God says that the fear of God is the beginning of wisdom. When intellect meets wisdom prosperity opens up. As we examine the book of Habakkuk the second chapter in verse one it says that *I will stand upon my watch and set me upon the tower, and will watch to see what he will say unto me, and what I shall answer when I am reproved. The key here is to get alone with God and wait for the Lord to give you the vision (the prophetic insight to your future).* The young man sad that he will stand on top of the tower and watch what the Lord will say to him. The Lord answered and said *write the vision, and make it plain upon tables, that he may run that readeth it.* If the young man had not sought after God for the vision he would not have gotten it. There has been numerous times I have jumped in a business without seeking the father and the end result was it did not work out. I have made thousands of dollars on some of the opportunities but yet they were short lived. The word says that the blessings of the Lord will overtake you. You can find yourself in a "rat race", always chasing the cheese instead of letting the cheese find you. The father went on to say in Habakkuk two *for the vision is yet for an appointed time, but at the end it shall speak, and not lie: though it tarry, wait for it; because it will surely come, it will not tarry.* As you begin to speak with father not only will he show you the vision but he will give you clear direction for his word will not return void. We can look in the book of Daniel and see that the Lord favored him. Why? He spent time with the father through fasting and prayer. God gave Daniel knowledge and intelligence in every branch of literature and wisdom. Daniel even understood all kinds of visions and dreams. The enemy through him in the Lion's den but yet he was saved because he had a relationship with the father. I want you to ponder for a moment... "*what if you had that relationship with God?* " The God of Heaven and Earth! The only created that knows the beginning to the end. O my God, to have insight, intelligence and outstanding wisdom. How many of us would have saved time, money and energy by simply seeking him first?

The enemy wants us to stay in the realm of *fear and intellect* not *intellect and wisdom*. In fact, fear causes us to abort the promise. He does not want us to have the promise. The word says if any man lack wisdom, you should ask God, who gives generously to all without finding fault, and it will be given to you. Wisdom is free to us. God said he will give wisdom to you. All you have to do is ask for it. Wisdom is our friend. In fact, the word says in the book of Proverbs that wisdom is our sister and call understanding your relative. I invite you now to stop what you are doing and say Father forgive me. Today I call wisdom my sister and understanding my kinswoman. Father open my eye of understanding and let wisdom and understanding meet me in every area of my life in Jesus Name! Father I need your wisdom in this hour in Jesus Name! Father sharpen my discernment and increase my capacity in Jesus Name! You see if you have sister wisdom and cousin understanding you can be successful in business and in life. *My advice to you "Wise Up & Rise Up" your time to take "Dominion"!*

Wisdom Affirmations

God give me the discernment to make sound decisions.

I am guided by divine wisdom in every thought, word and action.

My capabilities are enlightened with sister wisdom and cousin understanding.

I have the wisdom of King Solomon. My sister wisdom is a gift from God.

My sister wisdom increases my intuition.

My sister wisdom has made me a sage among my peers.

My sister wisdom gives me the ability to perceive, believe and proceed.

God give me knowledge and understanding so that I could gain wisdom through my experiences.

The two words of wisdom are --- pay attention.

ABOUT DR. JACQUELINE MOHAIR;

Her Excellency Rev Dr. Jacqueline Mohair was appointed to WOLMI/International Third World Leaders Association Ambassador to the United Nations (UN) Economic and Social Council (UNECOSOC) on January 26, 2015. The appointment of Ambassador was granted by The United Nations Headquarters in Geneva, Switzerland. Word of Life Christian Fellowship/Word of Life Ministries International is a Non-Governmental Organization (NGO) in special consultative status with the Economic and Social Council of the UN and the first Full Gospel Ministry granted consultative status with the UN. In her new role, Dr. Mohair will be responsible for the Global Empowerment of Women and Gender Equality in business and the Global Health Agenda of the United Nations Economic and Social Council (UNECOSOC). Her responsibilities will include reviewing some of the largest threats facing the world such as improving economic opportunities for women's health and girls. Her personal initiatives as Ambassador will include: - helping the UN further "The Road to Dignity 2030 Campaign" and it's priorities - to end poverty, - to transform lives, - to instill a degree of faith for all, She believes that everyone has the right to a standard of living adequate for their health and well- being. Dr. Mohair's efforts will include fostering partnerships betweenthe United Nations, private sector, foundations, community and government to maximize the outcomes for the world's most vulnerable people by identifying solutions to international economic, social and health challenges. Regarding being an ambassador, Dr. Mohair's perspective is of a socioeconomic responsible nature, believing that those who have more should be willing to assist those who have far less. Dr. Mohair, an entrepreneur, professor and author has written inspirational books on empowerment and entrepreneurship. Dr. Mohair is a personal branding strategist, business coach and professional speaker who is passionate about empowering people to succeed in life and business. An engaging and inspiring speaker and coach, her clients come away with a wealth of ideas that will make them better at their jobs and more effective at growing their businesses. With more than 17 years of marketing and sales experience, and 10 years as an entrepreneur, Jacqueline has helped hundreds of small business owners, corporate professionals, and non-profits succeed. Dr. Mohair's unwavering work ethic has enabled the development of multi-million dollar revenue producing companies. She serves as founder and CEO of Mpowered Media Solutions, a global business development firm that helps entrepreneurs create winning strategies for success. Dr. Mohair has a strong record of humanitarian service that includes operating as CEO/Founder of Heaven at New Haven Outreach, Inc. and an active member of Kingdom Life Worship Center. She obtained her Bachelor's in Business Administration with a minor in Marketing from Mississippi State University; attained a Masters in Educational Leadership from

Argosy University; a Masters in Internet Marketing from Full Sail University; a Doctorate of Ministry and Leadership from CICA International University & Seminary, a Honorary Doctorate Degree in Divinity, DBA-Candidate in Marketing from Argosy University and received numerous civic and private association awards. Her extensive international travel has helped to develop a great appreciation for all cultures, as reflected in her training sessions held worldwide. Dr. Jacqueline Mohair is President of Mpowered Media Solutions an extension of Mpowered Minds LLC. Prior to launching Mpowered Media Solutions, Dr. Mohair worked in corporate America for more than 15 year in Sales and Marketing. She has also reached the top position in 3 network-marketing companies. She partnered with companies such as Enron, SBC, Bellsouth, MCI-World Com and AT&T. She gained a wealth of knowledge pertaining to growing a business from the "grass roots" level and has mentored others on the skillset to attain success. As a result, she has earned numerous awards. She's married to His Excellency Rev. Dr. H.T. Mohair of 14 years and together they have 4 children and 4 grand-children.

Connect with Dr. Mohair,

(888) 400-8257

www.iciofhigherlearning.com

www.JacquelineMohair.com

CHAPTER THREE

⤸

Imagination

Sherlyn "Visionary" King

Imagination "Creation"

"The world inside your head is bigger than the world outside your head"
- Socrates

How did I come to believe in Network Marketing? I Know this women. She was working with her sisters and brother in the clothing industry at that time in her life. Her husband was very involved in Network Marketing during this period. She couldn't understand what network marketing was but she held on to her husband's belief.

Then one day she called her husband and told him she was experiencing chest pains. She drove herself to hospital and submitted to a series of tests. Later that evening the doctor entered the room and said, "YOU KNOW WHAT?! All your tests came back negative but they always over look young black woman, so I'm going to observe you overnight." That night, while under observation, the woman flat-lined for 6 seconds. The next morning she woke up unaware of the previous night's goings on. She was told she had to have emergency surgery to implant a pacemaker into her heart. She remembers saying to herself, "Thank You Jesus for save my life!!!" Her life had taken a turn because she couldn't go back to work. Although she was grateful for her life, she could not help but think of the things she could no longer do. Things that she loved and took for granted before. She remembers talking with a young man over the phone. That inspired her to stop dwelling on what happened to her. He told her, "God Just Made You Better." That statement changed her mind set and it was a relief to have those burdens lifted off of her mind. "I can do all things through Christ which strengtheneth me." Philippians 4:13. Although she did not understand the appeal of network marketing, she was, however, so thankful that her husband was involved with it as it kept a steady flow of income during this time. She remembered lying in hospital bed at home listening to her husband do conference call for the business he was in at the time. He spoke of a strategy called the PS3, which stands for; Peak interest, Show the plan, and 3way calls. At that point she began to take interest in what her husband was doing. She remembered pulling herself up through the pain she was experiencing and walked to his computer to see what her husband was doing. She remembers listening to Jim Rohn, "I am working full-time on my job and part-time on my fortune would you like to hear my story?" That resonated with her. She remembers telling her husband that she was supposed to do Network Marketing with him. Then they became business partners. Her husband brought her to an event and she remembers being in the audience looking at the people on stage speaking. At that moment she saw herself on stage speaking and inspiring people, it was like a Déjà VA moment! A shift happened for her. It was a life changing experience for her. This woman that I know personally is Me. .Meet Sherlyn King.

Ground floor

I am so happy and grateful to have this opportunity to share my amazing life-changing mental success steps with each and every visionary who reads this chapter. I truly believe this opportunity was God sent. I remember sharing with my husband, Silas King III that I was going to write a book a few years ago. I spoke it into the atmosphere back then and now to be sharing my golden nuggets of life-changing experience is simply breathtaking. I have a clear vision that I will make a difference in your lives and in mine. I've spoken it, I've written it down, I have abundant and unwavering faith, and I speak affirmations each day; stating and restating my vision as fact. It is through actions such as these that I've been blessed to be a part of this marvelous book. I am grateful for the opportunity to show you how to do the same.

"Success is based on Imagination plus ambition and the will to work."
- Thomas Edison

Everything starts with imagination. An idea forms in someone's mind and then they create it. *The Oprah Winfrey Show, Computers, and even Network Marketing Companies* all start out as an idea in someone's mind. The transition of getting an idea from your imagination to the real world is what we will touch on in this chapter. I want you to imagine your life as a six story building that contains four elevators. Each story of the building is a different life-lesson that will bring you closer to success once it is mastered. Currently, you occupy the ground floor, but you aspire to be on the rooftop. The ground floor symbolizes where you are now in your life. The rooftop represents the achievement of your goals and aspirations. Basically, the rooftop symbolizes your ideal vision of success. The elevators will be the vehicles that will transport you from where you are now to where you want to go. Each floor in the building will introduce a new lesson to ensure success. I am going to show you the blueprint of how to get from where you are now to where you want to be. Here and now, take a ride with me and your life will never be the same.

Oprah said, Only You can move your life forward.

HOPE

As our journey begins, we walk up to the elevators located in the heart of the building. There are four elevators numbered 1,2,3,4. There is a sign posted that states only odd numbered elevators can access the rooftop. I select the button to call an elevator. We hear a "DING!" and a distant voice calls out "Floor 1, Ground Floor". The doors open for the elevator to the far right, elevator 4. I see a slight twinge of disappointment in your eyes. In life, there are always going to multiple paths to get you where you want to be. Some of them will be direct, others will require a transit. Sometimes, you will need to use many methods to accomplish your goals. With that revelation, I see you perk up. We take a step inside, eager to start this journey to success. Although this elevator has no rooftop access, there is much to be said for what can be learned along the journey to success. I press the button for the second floor. As it illuminates, again we hear a voice call from the speaker located somewhere just beyond our view, "Next stop second floor; Hope". The elevator comes to a smooth halt and the door opens. This floor is dedicated to Hope.

The dictionary definition for hope is "A feeling of expectation and desire for a certain thing to happen". The first step to moving your life in a successful direction is to have hope. You have to have a burning desire and willingness to change your current situation. On top of that, you have to have the expectation that the things you desire will come to pass. The bible talks of hope often, however one passage, Proverbs 13:12, shows us that hope alone is not enough;

"Hope deferred makes the heart sick, but a longing fulfilled is a tree of life."

If one is hopeless then it will surely be not only detrimental to the success of that individual, it will also be detrimental to their quality of life. No one can live a happy life with a sick heart. Hope is a necessary component to success; however you must also put in the work to accomplish your goals. That is how you will truly be fulfilled and be granted with the ability to help fulfill others.

In addition to the traditional meaning of the word, hope can also be interpreted to stands for; Help Other People Everyday. If you are the only person that benefits from your dreams, then they are not big enough. Dream bigger! There is a whole world of lives out there that you can touch; that you can change. Each day you should be in search of people that you can help in some way. My dream includes being able to help you believe that you can achieve the life you picture. Continuing to have hope is the key to creating the life that you desire.

VISION: How Big Is Your Vision?

Now that you are hope-filled, we journey back to the elevator. I select the button to call an elevator. Again, the elevator to the far right opens. We step in and I press the button for the 3rd floor. That, now familiar, voice calls out, "Next stop third floor; Vision." A few seconds later the elevator doors slide open and we see a simple but powerful sign, on it, the words proclaim:

> *"Where there is no vision, the people perish*
> **-Proverbs 29:18"**

Internalize that statement. If you do not have a vision for your children, they will perish. If you do not have a vision for your health, it will perish. Likewise, if you do not have a vision of your success, then your goals too, will perish. It is time to enlarge your Vision. What does your vision look like? Think about it. What does it feel like? Feeling the feelings of already having it. Embrace It! Ask yourself; "What do I really want?" Whatever you want for your future, you must first imagine and it will manifest itself. Keep looking towards the prize and surely you will succeed.

The first step is to manifest a vision for your life. This is easier than it sounds, but it is surprising how many people lack vision. In order to create a vision you must first dream. A dream is an idea that is created in your imagination. Dreaming is not just something you do at night while sleeping. Day dreaming is a valuable tool when creating your vision. I know in school you were probably reprimanded for day dreaming and stopped the practice. However, I am here to tell you to reincorporate it into your life. I want you to dream with your eyes wide open. Dreaming is the fuel that shapes your vision. Your dreams should be so big that they scare everyone around you. People are going to think you are crazy but as Maya Angelou says, *"If you are always trying to be normal you will never know how amazing you can be"*. Use your imagination. Let it run wild. What is the biggest, craziest, most wonderful dream that you can dream? It is possible.

We don't think in words or phrases, we think in pictures, emotions, and images. *"No one ever made a great discovery without the exercise of the imagination." -George Henry Lewes.* When you remember an event; you picture it. When you are thinking of your future, images appear of what you believe it will look like. So it makes sense that if you see something for a prolonged time it gets into your subconscious mind. Every time you see your dream (with your physical eyes or your mind's eye) you have an emotional response in your spirit. As you look at your goals over and over, they are moving close to you. I have pictures all of my room because I truly believe that it works. You are making your subconscious hyperaware of that particular thing or goal and that will ultimately attract it to you. Have you ever had someone make you aware of a type of car that you'd never seen before, and then all of a sudden you see it everywhere? That is the same sort of law of attraction that you will be applying in every aspect of your life.

In 2014, I was blessed to host an incredible ladies event; Women with Vision. There were several highlights of that event, but for me, the best moment was when each attendee completed a vision board. Seeing the ladies transform their visions for their lives into a tangible object was breathtaking. Each woman in attendance created a concrete manifestation of what they wanted out of their life. How powerful is that? The ladies took their ideas and turned them into something they could view every day. A vision board is an important step in seeing your dreams come to fruition. I challenge each and every one of your to create a vision board today.

To create your very own vision board follow the steps listed below:

Steps to Creating a Vision Board

- Create a clear picture of what you want in your mind and write your aspirations in a journal.
- Go through magazines that inspire you and cut out pictures that represent your goals and that speak to your heart. Also gather pictures of yourself to include on your vision board.
- Arrange the pictures on a poster board.
- Hang your Vision board up so you can see it daily. Ideal places included your bedroom and hallways, in your restrooms, refrigerator, Front door, back door. All over your house. Look at it frequently.
- Spend time each day visualizing obtaining the goals and items on your board(s)

Your vision board will help you to focus. It serves as a constant reminder of what you are working towards. If you see it in your mind you can hold it in your hand. I remember creating a vision board years ago with my dream car, a Mercedes Benz S550. I spoke to my vision board every day. I would sit for a few moments in the morning and a few in the evening imagining what owning the car of my dreams would be like. I would go to the Dealership and take pictures of myself sitting in the driver's seat. Then one day, my husband called me to go dealership to get my dream car. I will never forget that moment drive off the parking lot with the S550 Mercedes Benz and two weeks after we got the Mercedes-Benz look on the wall of my dream board and I scream!!! Guest what…It was the same Mercedes-Benz that was in our driveway was on our Dream / Vision board on our bedroom wall. It was the most amazing feeling to be able to reach out and touch something that I had dreamed about for so long. If it can happen for me then it can happen for you too. As you accomplish the goals on your dream board, you can replace them with new goals or simply create an entire new dream board.

The future belongs to those who believes in the beauty of their dreams.
Eleanor Roosevelt

You must see the manifestation of your goals on the canvas of your imagination. Make your visualizations as clear as you possibly can. You must describe in detail what you want. Paint a picture so clear that the ocean waters of Maldives would be envious. Whether your goal is purchasing an automobile or to complete your doctorate, it is imperative to familiarize yourself with every aspect of achieving that goal. If your goal is to buy a Bugatti, then you must know the color of the car you desire both inside and outside. You must know how much the car costs. You should be able to visualize yourself driving it. What is playing on the radio? What are you wearing? How is the weather that day? You must go and take pictures in your dream car and include them on your dream board. Take the car for a test drive. You must be able to visualize yourself owning YOUR car. Doing these things will continually reaffirm your vision and keep you focused on your goal. Actions such as these are referred to as dream building. We will discuss more about dream building later, as it too is essential to success.

When you discover your vision it will inspire your energy and passion. Ecclesiastes 9:10 says, "Whatsoever thy hand findeth to do, do it with thy might; for there is no work, nor device, nor knowledge, nor wisdom, in the grave, whither thou goest." You have one life to live and you are capable of living the life you desire. Fill yourself with hope and then get a clear vision of your success. Everything you want will come looking for you. It is TRUE!!! You get what you picture. You have to become infatuated with your dreams and goals. Every morning when you wake up and right before you go to bed you should be focused on your vision. You should spend time throughout the day with your dream board visualizing the manifestation of your success. Here is a phrase that I repeat each night while envisioning my goals coming to fruition, "My Dreams and Goals are coming to reality. How it will be done is not my business, it's God's business." God has placed a divine purpose on my life. My purpose has become my passion. It wakes me up in the morning. It gives me (Joy/Peace/Fulfillment) no matter what obstacles I am facing. I know that what God has given me to accomplish cannot be stopped by anyone. I will finish strong! " You can replace the pronouns with your actual name for a more potent effect. This is an example of affirmations, which we will explore in more detail later. My desire is that you will be inspired, motivated, and challenge to get back in the race towards your dreams. I encourage you to get back the passion for fulfilling your goals. I want you to achieve God's purpose for your life because you deserve to live a life of your dreams.

For I know the plans I have for you," declares the LORD, "plans to prosper you and not to harm you, plans to give you hope and a future. Jeremiah 29:11

Belief/Fear

We head back to the elevators and select the button to call one. This time elevator number 2 opens. I see a sparkle in your eye. You are aware that this coach will not take us to our ultimate destination, but enthusiastic nonetheless as you now know that the journey is as important as that ultimate goal. Once inside, we select the option for the 4th floor. The voice, which is starting to sound very familiar, calls out, "4th Floor, Belief" The doors open to an amazing view. We are standing on a dock that opens up to mile and mile of clear blue sea. There are yachts surrounding the dock. You may think to yourself that a yacht is a strange setting to increase your belief and you may be right.

However, that was the very setting where I learned that the true key to accomplishing your goals is your belief level.

My husband and I were in Florida for the "**Retreat of a Lifetime**", an organized retreat that we qualified for a few years ago. As a treat we went on a Cruise on a yacht. The sights were breath taking but I

Found value in being able to speak with others who had accomplished goals similar to the ones that I was looking to achieve. I remember us speaking to one Multimillionaire on the cruise and we asked, "What makes you different from us?" I was at a loss. We were both hardworking and yet his income exceeded mine. After a few moments of silence he spoke up, "I believe more" he stated. That blew me away. That's it, I thought, believe more. I can do that! At that point you could have knocked me over with a feather. Immediately my mind was transformed. I adopted an "I can do that" attitude.

The next question was How Saying "I believe more" is one thing but actually doing it, increasing my belief level took work. I started reading and listening to every personal development CD and book that I could get my hands on. A few in particular really touched my heart and helped to change my way of thinking. **The Magic of Believing by Claude Bristol** was a selection that I read but also obtained the audio for it. There were wonderful teachings in that selection, such as; if you want to be great you must hang with great people. If you want to be successful, hang around successful people. If you want to awaken the genius inside you, then hang around people who are in touch with great ideas. I would allow the audio to play over and over, when I was driving or sleeping so those ideas could really seep into my psyche. I am a firm believer in growth. You do not know it all and you never will. All you know is what you know right now. But there is always room for growth and an opportunity to know more. That's why you got to feed your mind with personal development and by reading books. When you read and listen to personal development material, you are positioning yourself to realize and maximize your potential. You are increasing your belief in not only your goals but also in yourself. Here are a few of the books that I recommend.

Personal Development:

- *How to Win Friends and Influence People By Dale Carnegie*
- *Think and Grow Rich by Napoleon Hill*
- *Secret of the Millionaire Mind by T. HARV Eckerd*
- *The Magic of Thinking Big by David J. SCHWATZ.*
- *The Strangest Secret by Earl Nightingale*

Another system I learned to increase my belief level was to recite Affirmations. An affirmation is the action or process of affirming something or being affirmed. Another word for Affirmation is declaration. You can literally declare what you want in your life.

Anything that you can imagine for your future can be obtained. Affirmations are more powerful than you can ever imagine. One of my favorite quotes from *Ella Wheeler Wilcox is, "If your imagination is the mirror of your soul, then you have a perfect right to stand before that mirror and see yourself as you wish to be.* You have the right to see, reflected in that magic mirror, the mansion you intend to own, the factory you intend to manage, the bank of which you intend to be president, the station in life you intend to occupy." Your imagination belongs to you! Use it to become what and who you believe you are. Think how powerful that is. Anything that you can imagine you are able to affirm them with your words and soon it will become a firm belief in your heart. Once you believe it you can achieve it. As cliché as that sounds it is the absolute truth.

I want each of you to go to the mirror right now and say these affirmations:

I am who I say I am*I am blessed *I am God's creation* I am wealthy* I am a leader* I am confident* I am fearless* I am a Can Do Woman and CAN stands for Courage, Action, and Never Quitting* I am victorious* I am an overcomer* I am unstoppable* I am determined* I am full of joy* I am beautiful inside and out* I am intelligent* I have high Self-esteem* I am Liberated* I am a Money Magnet* I am walking on purpose*I am debt Free* I Am Masterpiece* I Am Prosperous* I Am Powerful and I Love It*I am Good Enough *I am Successful *I am a Winner* I am Daring *I have Vision *I am Excellent *I love me some me* *I am a woman that win* *I am Whole and Perfect as I was create.*

Create your own affirmations about what you want to have, do, be, see and experience. Your affirmations should be personal to you. They should be focused on increasing your self-belief and the realization of your vision. There are so many women that don't believe they are good enough. I am here to tell you that you are enough, period. You're a winner and a champion and you always hit your goals. Do NOT let anyone tell you that you are not good enough, smart enough, fine enough, well-spoken enough, likeable enough, or any other deficiency. Do not let anyone speak lack into your life. You are not lacking, you are good enough. I want you to step into your day and know your worth. I am talking to you. There are going to be times when you feel like you have been doing your best and it's not getting you where you want to be in business or your personal relationships, but you just have keep speaking your affirmations and, believing in your dreams and in yourself. You are something special. The obstacles that you are facing serve a purpose.

Whether it is to teach you a lesson, make you stronger, teach you to lean on God, or increase you belief, there will be a purpose to your trials.

The more I thought about that Multimillionaire on the yacht, the more his words rang true. Achieving your goals and success is directly related to your belief level. If he could have all the things his heart desired and I have been able to achieve my goals, then you too are capable of the same. Repeat after me:

I can decide all that is possible for anyone is possible for me. I am successful. I am full of the power of success. That is a simple truth.

- Unknown

You have to make the conscience decision that nothing is beyond your grasp. You have to believe that you are capable of any and all things. You have to face your deepest fears head on. From here on out, fear is going to stand for false evidence appearing real. You are a fear Eliminator. One of my favorite quoted on fear is from Anthony Robbins, *"Life is found in the dance between your deepest desire and your greatest fear".* Fear is a part of life but it is not a part of success. You have to be willing to step out on faith and you have to be willing to fail. If you have a fear of failure it is very likely that you will not achieve your goals. In 2006, I was afraid to speak in front of an audience. Actually I was terrified. I remember my husband calling me to the front of an audience to share my 'Why letter'. This is letter that I wrote to explain why I was determined to win in the business we were in. I remember standing in front of the crowd holding my letter with both hands and shaking. My knees, my hands, and my voice were all shaking. But you know what? I did it anyway. I cannot remember what I said and I am not even sure that my thoughts were cohesive, but I do know one thing; I finished. I faced my greatest fear in that moment. I finished and it didn't kill me. I was terrible but no one laughed. After I was done and had stumbled to my seat sever people came up to me and told me how I had inspired them with my passion. One person even had tears in their eyes. I had spent so much of my life afraid to speak to large crowds when in truth; it is a part of my calling. I may not always have the right words but my passion stands firm. People can feel it. Had I allowed my fears to control my actions I may never have discovered this side to myself. And let it be with you. There are many special gifts and talents buried deep within you. They are buried just beyond the fear. Belief is all it takes to conquer your fears and unlock that talent. Visualize yourself not as you are but as you can be.

Dream Building

We are fearless, we know that each and every dream that we can fathom will inspire a vision that we will be able to achieve. We are hopeful and believe and any and everything that our heart desires is within our grasp. With these truths planted firmly in our hearts we venture back to the elevators. This time before I can reach out to call one, I see your hand shoot out and press the call button. Good, you are finally taking control of your journey. Elevator 2 opens to allow us passage. I glance over and there is not a bit of frustration on your face. You're getting it. Each floor (life's journey) holds value. It is not always about going directly to the rooftop. We step into the elevator and again you beat me to the "push". You select the 5th floor. The voice on the speaker is becoming noticeably more familiar. It calls out, "5th floor, Dream Building".

This, by far is my favorite floor. All the other floors are about doing important work within yourself to prepare you for success and attracting success to you. Dream building has similar outputs but the work is more physical. Although intangible qualities such as imagination are still needed, you will increase your belief level through somatic activities. We have covered many of these activities in other sections, such as writing down your dreams/visions, creating vision boards, and even going on a go-see; to "go- see" your vision come to reality. Examples of go-sees are going to your dream home, visiting the auditorium where graduation is held, or even visiting the location where you will open your business. Affirmations can also be great tools in dream building.

You must see the end before the Beginning. You have to be able to visualize yourself accomplishing the goals that you set forth. Before you even begin on the path you have to know how it will end. You may not know how you will get to that end place, but the end needs to be clear. For some people this task can be difficult and that is where your dream building techniques come into play. It may be difficult for you to visualize owning your dream home. When things are difficult to picture there is no way we can formulate a plan to achieve that goal. We think of it as unattainable. However, if you write that dream in your journal, then begin to speak affirmations regarding it, place of picture of the home on your dream board, and go to a few open houses, then all of a sudden that unattainable dream is a clad iron vision. Doing these things not only increases your belief level but they also increase your knowledge. Imagine how much I could learn from the realtors at the open houses or from an online article that you accessed to get a picture for your dream board. Information is a major factor in being able to actually obtain a goal. Dream building does just that, building your dream from a simple idea to something achievable.

Timing Is Everything

We walk back to the elevators. You select the button to call one. Elevator 3 opens. Finally, an odd elevator! We could bypass the final floor and go straight to the rooftop. I wait to see what you will do. You select the 6th floor. I smile to myself because you've realized just what that floor is going to teach you; Timing is everything. Imagine if the first coach had taken us directly to the rooftop. How long would we have been able to maintain success; being hopeless, with no vision, having a lack of belief, and no tools to dream build?

I remember when I was younger in my own self-actualization journey, my husband would put personal development audio on in the car and I would literally cover my ears. I did not want to hear it. Can you imagine me, a grown woman, sitting in the car with my hands over my ears repeating, "Lalalalalalalalala", to drown out the sound of life changing material. I wasn't ready. I thought personal development was boring. How could some rich person who knew nothing of my struggle tell me how to be a better me and achieve my dreams? And why would I sit there and listen to them tell me it was my fault that I wasn't successful? That was my train of thought in that period of my life. I was defensive because I was insecure. Instead of opening myself up to learn from people who had accomplished the things that I wanted to accomplish, I shut myself off because I felt judged. I wasn't ready. I felt judged by an audio tape. Think how silly that sounds. The people on the tape were saying things that hit close to home and instead of owning my truth I deflected by sticking my fingers in my ears or complaining the tapes were boring. I was not ready for that level of thinking or the growth involved. Someone telling me that my success hinged on my ability to believe in myself was mind blowing. I took offense to that train of thought because I wasn't ready to accept responsibility for my own success and wealth. I had to grow out of that mindset and realize that my successes and failures begin and end with me. It is important to remember that God presents us with the right opportunities when we are ready for them. Everything in your past has brought you to this moment. This is your time. Had you read this book five years ago it would not have had the same impact as it does right now. In this very moment, you are ready. Go out and conquer.

Roof Top

The time is now! We are now running back to the elevator, excited to know that we are one floor away from our destination. You press the call button and elevator 1 opens. We leap in and immediately press the button for the rooftop. As the elevator rises, the walls fade and are replaced by glass. Still encompassed within the elevator, a scenic panoramic image comes into view. The roof top is everything you've ever imagined it to be. We hear the voice once again, "Rooftop, you have arrived." Then it clicks, the reason this voice has been so familiar is because it is your voice. You didn't recognize it at first, but it has been there guiding you to your destination. Trust yourself; you know what you are doing.

You have an opportunity to create your legacy. Look back on your life and all that you've been through and ask yourself 'have I truly made a difference in this world?' If the answer is yes, great! But there is still work to do. If the answer is no, then there is still time. Anything and everything that you can dream of, is possible. Let your dreams shape the vision for your life, speak life into your visions through affirmations, dream build, release you fear and believe that any and everything is possible when the time is right. IMAGINE! BELIEVE! RECEIVE! And never quit. You dream could be right over that last hurdle that you decide not to jump or just beyond that valley that you decide it is not worth it to cross. Nobody can write the way you do. Nobody can speak the way you do. Nobody can create the way you do. You are powerful. You are confident. You are successful.

You look up and you see that the roof top wasn't the final destination at all. Your building is connected to several other taller buildings with ladders. You take a moment to enjoy your success and then head off in the direction of those ladders motivated to conquer new levels with the lessons you've learned from this part of your life and the lessons to come.

"Go confidently in the direction of your dreams. Live the life you have imagined."

-Henry David Thoreau

Quotes :

"Vision without action is just a dream. Action without vision is simply passing the time. Action with vision can change world." - **Joel Barker**

"Knowledge is limited. Imagination in encircles the world."
- **Albert Einstein**

"Everything you can imagine is real." - **Pablo Picasso**

"As a man thinks in heart, so is he." - **Proverbs 23:7**

"All our dreams can come true if we have the courage to purse them."
-**Walt Disney**

"Nothing happens unless first a dream" - **Carl Sandburg.**

"Commit to the Lord whatever you do and your plans will succeed." -
Proverbs 16:3

"If you can conceive and believe it, you can achieve it."
- **Napoleon Hill**

Affirmations:

Speak: I Am Her. Affirmations Daily:

A Super woman...I Am Her A Strong woman...I Am Her A Spiritual woman...I Am Her

A Sophisticated woman ...I Am Her A Vision woman....I Am Her A Faith woman...I Am Her

A Fearless woman....I Am Her

A Multi-Millionaire woman...I Am Her A Confidence woman...I Am Her

A Masterpiece Woman... I Am Her

Catch your success it's near.

- Sherlyn King

ABOUT SHERLYN KING

Sherlyn King is married to a God Fearing Man and they have 4 Children and 4 beautiful grandchildren. She Love's the Lord with all her Heart. She inspires others to believe more. Sherlyn was introduced to network marketing in September of 2006. Being a Successful Entrepreneur, She is also a woman with a huge heart and vision. She has a passion and purpose to help millions of women around the world to be successful and to let go of the spirit of fear. She has appeared in the Gold Standard Magazine with her husband. She is a Motivational speaker, Visionaire Encourager Coach, and she believes in having a "Millionaire Mindset". "WHAT YOU THINK ABOUT. YOU BRING ABOUT."

Sherlyn's charisma has impacted many lives. She had a chance to speak in front of 20,000 people. She has impacted audiences with her life changing story. She teaches others to Believe Bigger and Faster. She is a handbag designer. She holds a Nursing degree. She has excelled in the Clothing Industry as a top sales woman. She knows how it feels to live the #1 lifestyle in the world. She truly believes in living the dream life.

She has a heart of a champion and she paint's her dream every moment. Some of Sherlyn's biggest influences are her husband Silas King III, John Maxwell, Joyce Meyer and Jim Rohn, she said," "One of the greatest gifts you can give to anyone is the gift of attention". Sherlyn's whole goal is to make a difference. Sherlyn King is an inspiration to her women group "Ladies with Vision". She always dreams of a better life and to help other to JUST WIN...

Her dad always told her..."Your name means Something Great."

Her mom inspired her to listen more than talking and believe in yourself worth.

Sherlyn states that her inspiration is her husband Silas King III and their four beautiful children, Ledrena Richardson, Rekita King, Demonay King and Silas King IV.

Special thanks to Rekita King for her help in making this chapter possible with her amazing gift of editing.

You can learn more about Sherlyn King by visiting her website below:

Sherlyn King
832-978-8397
Email: www.onebillionsb@yahoo.com Facebook:
Www.facebook.com/Sherlyn.King.7 Twitter:
www.twitter.com/onebillionsb
Instagram: w ww.instragram.com/iamsherlynking
www.totallifechanges.com/health4kingwealth

I BELIEVE IN YOU!!!!

CHAPTER FOUR

❧

Gifts and Talents

Prophetess Joyce Stewart

Gifts and Talents

Upon first glance, gifts and talents always appeared to be one and the same and many use these terms interchangeably. Perhaps it is possible to substitute them, depending upon the context given.

However, for the purpose of making a distinction and to bring enlightenment of their uniqueness I will make mention of their differences.

As a young girl, I was precocious and very curious growing up as an "only child". My play dates were few and that lead to a lot of mental activity or a "vivid imagination" as one may call it.

I read more than the average child my age, was very chatty, I daydreamed a lot and was overly sensitive in my emotions - as far as adults were concerned. Later on all of these behaviors were perceived as a negative and I was very misunderstood because of my inability to rightly communicate my feelings without extreme outbursts of emotion.

During my preteens through early teens I fancied becoming a singer. I loved performing and dancing around my parents friends and would spent countless hours singing karaoke style prior to knowing that there was a such a name for it.

The only problem with the love and passion that I had for singing was no one else seemed to care about it as much as I did. It became just a cute performance that allowed me to side step my bedtime every now and then.

This was a talent, a natural ability that was not truly being acknowledged or encouraged in a serious way. As a result, my own doubts and insecurities crept in and I never pursued it. This is not a blame game to my parents because they obviously didn't know that it was important. Most parents of their generation put more emphasis on the traditional educational system.

The scripture (proverbs 22:6)– "Train up a child in the way they should go" is used more as a guideline for moral conduct and making sure church values are in place, it's not typically associated in the talent category as it should be.

TALENT

A talent is the result of a person's genetics and/or training.

Matthew 25:25 So I was afraid and went out and hid your gold in the ground. See, here is what belongs to you.

This was a talent I buried and after that - life had very little meaning to me. As a society at whole there are billions of people living aimlessly day after day without any true life purpose. They are missing out on the fundamental reason of why they are here.

The parable of the talents mentions that the one that you have will be taken if it is not used properly, Matthew 25:25.

After leaving home, I decided to go into the military, I got married and had two beautiful children. My life just didn't seem right. I was always unsatisfied and I felt it was my husband's responsibility to make me happy. When my marriage failed, I became my worst nightmare – a single parent.

Time went on and through the good, the bad and the ugly, I decided that I had had enough and gave my life over to God and asked Jesus to save me. It was the best decision that I made. I joined a church and was assigned what they called a "Care group leader".

This brave woman decided to mentor me!

Why is this all relevant or important? It was only when someone took an interest in me that my buried talents began to become unearthed.

All of my hidden emotions began to well up through my talent to write. First, it was a poem. I thought it was a fluke. I had never even enjoyed reading poems earlier in life so I was amazed that this ability to write increased the more I yielded myself to it.

As I became more comfortable in this new found talent, I began framing my poems and doing customized poetry and selling them as occasional gifts (Christmas, birthdays, etc.)

I was quickly becoming known around my friends, relatives and co-workers as a poet. It was like life had purpose and I was discovering who I was for the first time.

As I continued to learn more through the teachings in the word of God, I was becoming exposed to the "prophetic ministry" and would periodically receive a "word of knowledge" or a "prophesy" about my personal life or direction for what God had planned for me.

One prophet told me that as I considered becoming a paralegal that I should consider taking the bar as God had higher plans for me. I did become a paralegal but I was still so insecure in my abilities so I never went to law school even though I see now why I should have pursued it.

The point of the matter is that I really started to blossom in another talent that God was graciously restoring in me. Now this of course was only the beginning. Fast-forwarding 20-something years later after two prophetic mentors, I started to grow spiritually and now God was revealing my spiritual gifts.

Gifts

These are spiritual abilities that you are born with to use for God's Kingdom purpose(s).

1 Corinthians 12:1, 4-11

12 Now about the gifts of the Spirit, brothers and sisters, I do not want you to be uninformed.

⁴ There are different kinds of gifts, but the same Spirit distributes them.
⁵ There are different kinds of service, but the same Lord.

⁶ There are different kinds of working, but in all of them and in everyone it is the same God at work.

⁷ Now to each one the manifestation of the Spirit is given for the common good. 8 To one there is given through the Spirit a message of wisdom, to another a message of knowledge by means of the same Spirit, 9 to another faith by the same Spirit, to another gifts of healing by that one Spirit, 10 to another miraculous powers, to another prophecy, to another distinguishing between spirits, to another speaking in different kinds of tongues, and to still another the interpretation of tongues. 11 All these are the work of one and the same Spirit, and he distributes them to each one, just as he determines.

From a young child, I had always fantasied about heaven, angels and the supernatural. I didn't grow up in the church – so I was open minded about spiritual truths. That at times proved to make me vulnerable to error but on the positive side, I wasn't a religious person filled with a traditional mindset.

With a true hunger for reading the bible concerning prophets, healing and casting out spirits; it sounded to me like an amazing sci-fi action movie and I longed to see this God manifest himself to me in these ways.

However, nothing that is worth having is ever easy to obtain. I studied and learned from the best and with an earnest desire to grow – the Lord began to stir up my spiritual gifts as the gifts of prophecy, word of knowledge and intercession. At first, I was extremely skeptical about having these types of gifts because I believed that they should work in the manner that I envisioned on television or movies. I expected to have all these open faced visions and be beamed up like "Scottie" in star trek to heaven. I thought surely if Elijah, Ezekiel and Jeremiah were seeing angels and going on heavenly retreats that I should be too, right? Well, I believe that God can and will when it's the time and purpose to do those types of things but I've learned that God is more concerned with us developing our personal relationship with him first and foremost.

Now going back to my talents, I only discovered the writing when I had moments of alone time and I recommend meditating for those who may not even know any of their talents. God is very patient with his children and even though I have not yet used my singing abilities they will not be wasted as I love to worship and praise the Lord with my voice. He has reminded me on a few occasions that He never meant for me to become a "shower singer". Still God's mercy is extensive to the degree that He places us with the right individuals and the perfect atmosphere to develop and cultivate the gifts and talents.

Also keep in mind that the things I was put down for were the very things that lead to my gifts and talents being used. I was talkative because God had a call on my life to preach /teach/counsel, I daydreamed a lot because it was good for my writing, I was overly sensitive because of my prophetic nature and prophets are always misunderstood and rejected early on in life.

Altogether, my talents were at least 5 – not including my gifts: to teach, to lead, to counsel, to sing and to write. I don't believe this book being chapter 5 is by coincidence. The number five represents grace and boy did God give me plenty of it. In Genesis 1:22 he blessed the earth telling nature to be fruitful and multiply. It's also not by chance or an accident that my birthday is the 14th of July – again the number equals 5 for my day and 7 is the perfect number for completion. Many times in life we take our lives for granted. God made the system of Numbers, Satan just perverted it.

There was a season in my life that I was being instructed frequently to write "the book" by various prophets. I was confused about what book that God was referring to. I had no clue and did not feel that I was qualified or had any specific expertise to write on any particular subject. But how many of us know that God will use our life experiences whether it be "painful or joyful" to fit into our life's assignment, Romans 8:28 28 And we know that all things work together for good to them that love God, to them who are the called according to his purpose.

As I mentioned before, I was a highly imaginative child and that afforded me a lot of untapped stories for fiction. I had so much in me that I had learned from my own mistakes concerning love relationships, encouraging and supporting friends and my love for reading. This was the platform that enabled me to draw out the novel that became my first self-published work in July 2012, "The BBQ: Fireworks Spark."

I was ecstatic that I had finally done something that I felt was an accomplishment similar to climbing Mount Everest. Still, I was also growing in many other ways through the Holy Spirit, I was starting to counsel, teach and use my prophetic gift on a greater scale. The more effort I put in the more mature the gifts and talents grew.

What am I saying? God has fashioned us to come here in the earth with prepackaged gifts and talents. He meant for us to be equipped, so that in the day that He calls us to the forefront we can be ready to help, instruct and minister to others.

The bible says in Proverbs 18:16 New American Standard Bible A man's gift makes room for him, And brings him before great men.

What God's saying here is if you want to have influence in life it is your gift that will provide the way. Daniel had a spiritual gift to interpret dreams and that gave him an audience with a King. Prior to his gift - even being realized - it was his innate talent to be wise that lead him to be chosen to have the opportunity to be in the right place at the right time.

This is actually the whole conclusion – that in order to fulfill your purpose in life you must find out what your gifts and talents are. Without this knowledge it would be impossible to prosper or be used for the reason you were born.

Ephesians 2:10

For we are God's workmanship, created in Christ Jesus for good works, which God prepared in advance as our way of life.

This is reinforcing that he gave us a work, an assignment that through our gifts and talents we can make a living and be successful.

Let me show you another way, in the book of Timothy he exhorts the body of Christ in this manner:

1 Timothy 4:14

Do not neglect the spiritual gift you received through the prophecy spoken over you when the elders of the church laid their hands on you. So if you're unsure, go to your leaders and have those who are gifted through either the spirit of prophesy or wisdom to lay hands through faith to stir up the gifts. This is why I remind you to fan into flames the spiritual gift God gave you when I laid my hands on you, 2 Timothy 2:6.

So looking back now you have in the book of Matthew 25:25 a strong rebuke for someone who does not use their gift; and in 1 Timothy 4:14 he's instructing us not to ignore or count it lightly of the gift/call that God has placed on our lives.

Why is this such of importance? This is the very reason that you were born. God never creates anything or anyone without gifts or talents.

If for some reason you are one of God's children that has not discovered their gift/talents than the bible says to ask, seek and knock. These things are not meant to be secrets or mysteries to us as they contain your prosperity, wealth and whole existence.

Can you imagine not knowing the purpose of a stove, an iron or a television? They would go to waste or become invaluable because we wouldn't have any use for them. God forbid we would become unworthy of the call that was mandated before you were placed in the belly of your mother.

Jeremiah 1:4-5 The Call of Jeremiah

[4] The word of the Lord came to me, saying,

[5] "Before I formed you in the womb I knew you, before you were born I set you apart; I appointed you as a prophet to the nations."

As you read the next verse, just like Moses, Jeremiah began to explain to God (who made him) how unprepared he was and a list of excuses. Whatever, your excuse could be it has already been written in the books of heaven what you would become and God does not change his mind, He waits for you to change yours.

It is my greatest desire and to see others fulfill their destiny. "Destiny is not by chance but it is a matter of choice" (my old Bishop used to say this constantly). You must decide to press toward the mark for the prize of the high calling of God in Christ Jesus, Philippians 3:14.

I am ever so grateful of God's grace to be the author of my life because He wrote a story that has a happy ending. He has provided me with talent(s) to be a great influence: an author, a play writer, director, YouTube talk show host, motivational speaker, mentor, teacher and minister in training. All of these gifts and talents were revealed later on in my life which is proof that your age does not define your purpose.

I pray that you would be so compelled to see yourself with new eyes. I hope that you will go easy on you and forgive others if they have delayed you and forgive yourself for missing the mark. You can do all things through Christ who will strength you.

Your gifts and talents are Gods "money back guarantee" for a prosperous lifestyle.

3 John 2 Amplified Bible (AMP)

²Beloved, I pray that in every way you may succeed and prosper and be in good health [physically], just as [I know] your soul prospers [spiritually].

You may be wondering, how can I become prosperous in my soul? Using your talent(s) means you are no longer merely existing, living the mentality of a nine-to-fiver, and barely making it working at a job. You now have purpose and you are strengthened in your mental state by doing what you love. Whatever you love – drives you to become prosperous. This makes you whole in your soul and supports healing to your physical being.

Your gift used consistently (in conjunction with a personal relationship with the Holy Spirit) will produce fruit in your life and you will grow spiritually. Your hunger for God will cause you to develop an intimate walk with Jesus, the Holy Spirit and the Father. This entails becoming a mature believer and ultimately, this is the essence of true prosperity.

I thank God for making me into the woman I am today, my gifts & talents have truly blessed me but more so the body of Christ.

Remember this always: 1 Corinthians 14:1 Pursue love, and earnestly desire the spiritual gifts, especially that you may prophesy.

Your gifts and talents are in great demand! God Bless you on your journey.

ABOUT JOYCE C. STEWART:

Known for her poetry, plays, talk show host of YouTube Channel "Brides and Wives" and founder of The Love Business, has been a mentor, wise counsel to men and women needing a helping hand in the area of relationships especially in the love category. It is no wonder that she delves effortlessly into her "Edgy Christian love stories" which have been called captivating, realistic and teachable tools to use in everyday dating situations. Joyce uses her sense of humor to encourage others to consider their choices and consequences of waiting for the right kind of love - in a teachy but not preachy Christ-Inspired setting. Her first debut in 2012 for the first book, The BBQ: Fireworks Spark was well received. Since that time, book two The BBQ: Lover's Holiday its sequel stirred up even more excitement. Joyce is more than a romance novelist but also travels to do speaking engagements and women conferences (upon request).

Watch for the third edition of "The BBQ trilogy" Fall/Winter of 2015.

Connect with Joyce Stewart:

Facebook: Author Joyce Stewart

Facebook: The Love Business

Facebook: Best Friends Forever

Youtube Channel: Brides & Wives

Twitter: @Prophetbutterfly

Instagram: Author_Joyce_Stewart

CHAPTER FIVE

❧

Renewed Mindset

Bridgette Renee

Renewed Mindset

When I was asked to do this chapter I was shocked and nervous at the same time. I was immediately intimidated because I wasn't well known and thought I really didn't have anything profound to say. What could I possibly say to help change someone's thought process? I pray that those of you reading this will find something in my experiences to help change your mindset.

Don't Be A Victim....Be Prosperous in Your Thinking

I was a professional at this and didn't realize it. I had "daddy" issues and I had experienced physical, mental, and sexual abuse so throughout my life I played the victim role well. I didn't get enough attention from my father so I was going to cling to the next man I ended up in a relationship with and let the fact that he said he loved me validate me. Since I was abused before I'm going to look for the man who (even though he has a temper....RED FLAG) will protect me. I was neglected as a kid so this man saying he wants to marry me is validating me because finally I feel "good enough."

At almost 40 years of age is when I had to take a long hard look at my life and say "that's why you chose him." I didn't just wake up with that revelation, I was separated from my now exhusband and while I was going to God saying "You need to change him" God began showing me my issues and baggage and I realized I didn't have it as together as I thought I did! I had to put on my big girl pants and be accountable for my issues. I could hear God plain as day saying "You didn't pay attention to the signs!" "Those red flags were me telling you this is not a good fit for you but you ignored them and now you're experiencing the consequences!" I can hear the song by Kellee Patterson, If It Don't

Fit Don't Force It, playing over and over in my mind because that's exactly what I was trying to do in all of my relationships.

I had to take accountability for my issues and make a conscious decision to no longer be a victim. I had to choose to let go of the anger and bitterness because while I was holding on to all of that baggage and being miserable, the people who had hurt me were moving along just fine!

Holding on to all of that baggage will stunt your mental growth and hold you captive. I was holding on to all of that while putting up a front and attempting to portray myself as though I had it all together. You will never arrive at your full potential holding on to baggage because there will be no room for growth. You've hoarded all of those old feelings and now change can't happen because you refuse to let go. I was hesitant about letting things go because that meant I was freeing those people from what they had done to me and in my head every time I saw them I wanted them to remember! When I decided I was tired of being the "Bag Lady"(Erykah Badu) I knew that I had to mentally free everyone who had ever hurt me and in the process I freed myself! I didn't realize I wasn't operating at my full potential until this change happened. I'm blessed because I have a man and woman of God who have helped me along the way through prayer and teaching. Prayerfully those of you reading this already have that covering and if not I pray that God will lead you to where you need to be and place the right people in your lives. I didn't realize how happy I could truly be until this change happened. I was in a mental prison and when I was released I had a whole new outlook on life! I realized I don't have to be a victim, I don't have to be identified by what I went through, while my past made me the woman I am it doesn't define me and neither should yours. You deserve to be free, you deserve to operate in your full potential and you deserve to be happy so break the bondage of being a victim and become the Victor! BE PROSPEROUS IN YOUR THINKING!!!! The steps below helped me and hopefully you will be able to take something from my experience and apply it to your journey to becoming one with God and having a prosperous mindset!

ASSESSMENT

You cannot walk in prosperity in your thinking without at first assessing/acknowledging where you are right now. Where am I and how did I get here? The first step I took into becoming prosperous in my thinking was to assess where I was mentally and this is one of the hardest steps because it made me realize I did not have it all together like I wanted myself and everyone else to think when they saw me. It's a huge eye opener when you realize you are not all that you think you are and that you have a lot of stuff you need to work on.

ACCOUNTABILITY

The second step in my journey to becoming one with God and having a prosperous mindset was accountability. Ladies this is definitely the hardest step, at least it was for me! I had to take accountability for my actions and behavior that assisted me in getting to the place I was mentally. I had been operating in victim/ woe is me mode, unknowingly for so long that when my marriage was about to end I was praying to God that he would change him! I was in for a rude awakening because that's not how God operates! Instead he started to show me my issues that I had been holding on to and began showing me what I needed to change. The very first thing he showed me was my unresolved "daddy" issues. My father didn't have a consistent/active role in my life while I was growing up so I felt neglected. Having a man that wanted to be in a relationship with me meant that I was good enough, I was worthy and that I was special. These were the things I needed to feel from my father. Along with being told I was beautiful these were some of the things I had longed to hear from a man because I desperately needed to feel validated. Ladies this does not mean that I settled for just anyone. I called myself trying be selective but in the end it didn't work because, unbeknownst to me at the time, I was looking for the men that I chose to be with to make me feel like I was it! Like I was the show nuff stuff! Like I was the bomb diggity! Like God had broken the mold when he made me!

I did not realize that I should feel like that about myself before I even got into a relationship. Not conceited but feeling confident and secure. I could put up a good front like I was confident and secure but deep down I was still that self-conscious, insecure little girl. Don't be foolish like I was and convince yourself it's everyone else and you didn't play a part in it.

Proverbs 12:15 – The way of a fool is right in his own eyes: but he that hearkeneth unto counsel is wise.

FORGIVENESS

The next step is forgiveness. If the people that hurt you never apologized you still need to forgive them for your sanity and wellbeing. You're upset and moping with your lip stuck out, not being able to function in your daily life and those people are going on with their lives happy and living their lives.

As we get older and more mature in the word we realize it is not our job to enforce vengeance on those who hurt us. I was secretly hoping God would strike those people down and then I would feel better! Well, God never struck them down and while I was secretly hoping for it he began to ask me "Well what if I struck you down when you did this or that even though you repeatedly told me you would never do it again?"

Matthew 6:14-15 For if ye forgive men their trespasses, your heavenly Father will also forgive you:

But if ye forgive not men their trespasses, neither will your Father forgive your trespasses.

CHANGE YOUR THINKING

This step is a challenge because once you've operated in a particular way all of your life to just up and change it can be very difficult. *Romans 12:2 And be not conformed to this world: but be ye transformed by the renewing of your mind, that ye may prove what is that good, and acceptable, and perfect, will of God.*

Renewing of my mind is what I had to do. I had to make up in my mind that I was not going to wallow in my past and continue to allow myself to be in cruise control on the victim highway. I needed to make an exit and fast! This didn't happen overnight. It takes much prayer, fasting and studying the word.

One of the things that needed to change was anytime anyone brought up my divorce or anything else I had been through, if the conversation wasn't to glorify God then the conversation needed to be ended. All it takes is that one girlfriend to say "Girl I can't believe he did that" and before you know it you're caught back up in all those emotions and feelings you had before you made the decision to change your mindset. I would feel myself getting anxious and upset all over again so I had to constantly remind myself "Bridgette you are over that and that is part of your past so you need to move forward"! I have mentioned my divorce more than once because honestly, had it not been for the divorce and my experiences with my previous relationships I might not have gotten to the point to even realize I needed to change.

You have to also surround yourself with positive people because the more you hear the positivity little by little it will start to rub off on you. You can hear a conversation and you'll pick up a nugget of positivity here and there and you can start to apply it to your everyday life. Once you start to confess it you'll start to believe it!!

Jeremiah 29:11 *For I know the thoughts that I think toward you, saith the Lord, thoughts of peace, and not of evil, to give you an expected end.*

OPERATE IN YOUR PROSPEROUS THINKING

Once you've assessed where you are, taken accountability for your actions and changed your thinking you can move forward from your "stinkin thinkin" into having a prosperous mindset. Just because you've taken these steps doesn't mean you won't occasionally have a setback. I wish I could tell you once my mindset was changed that was it and I never went back to my old way of thinking. I'm a living witness that if you don't continue to maintain your new mindset you can easily find yourself stuck in a rut again. You have to make a conscious decision and say "No I'm not going to listen to that" or "I'm not that person anymore, that's the old me." As I stated earlier, when your best friend or anyone brings up what so and so did you need to shut the conversation down immediately because it's very easy to jump back on that train of "I can't believe they……………..and before you know it the peace and freedom you once had is now gone. So as soon as anyone brings whatever it is up just politely tell them, "that's a part of my past and that's where it is going to stay!" Don't get me wrong, if you're sharing you're experience with someone to show how you overcame then by all means share your experience but to be sitting around dwelling on it is something totally different. While I know everyone else's journey may be different from mine the ultimate goal is getting you to where you need to be so if you have to take a little from my experience and a little from someone else's the ultimate goal is you becoming one with God and changing your thinking.

Some days you may end up talking to yourself reminding yourself "Yes I went through that but that's in the past and I'm a new person!" There are numerous sites with daily affirmations on them. Find what applies to your particular circumstance and write them down on sticky notes if you have to and stick them throughout your house and confess them on a regular basis. In the midst of my change God has restored my relationship with my father and it is better than I could have ever imagined!!!

Job 22:28 *says to decree a thing and it shall be established! Decree that you will no longer have the same mindset! This along with the few steps I've mentioned should definitely get you started in the right direction on the road to having a prosperous mindset.*

Philippians 2:5

Let this mind be in you, which was also in Christ Jesus.

Ephesians 4:22 -24

22 That ye put off concerning the former conversation the old man, which is corrupt according to the deceitful lusts;

23 And be renewed in the spirit of your mind;

24 And that ye put on the new man, which after God is created in righteousness and true holiness.

ABOUT BRIDGETTE RENEE

Bridgette Renee was born and raised in Oklahoma. After numerous failed relationships, at the age of 38 she found herself divorced and having to start all over again. It was through that divorce that God began dealing with her on her issues and her life began to change. She credits the woman she is today to her mother, Doretha Seals, and her four sisters Alicia, Tara, Angela and MeChelle. She credits her family for being awesome examples and for being her backbone.

She enjoys reading and helping others. Bridgette Renee' has been employed with the Department of Defense for 14 1⁄2 years and through that employment God has blessed her to get paid for doing what she loves doing and that's catering to and serving other people and making sure all of their needs are met. She is an active member of Transformation Church International in Oklahoma City and falls under the leadership of Dr. Clarance and Pastor Tanya Johnson. She also volunteers and is the Executive Assistant for Covenant Couples ministry.

CHAPTER SIX

~

Women and Finance

Brenda Stroman

Woman and Finance

Did you know it is God's will for His children to prosper? Ladies, that includes us! Some people including Christians still believe it is an act of humility to be poor. They even quote or more accurately, misquote the Bible when they say, "Money is the root of all evil".

That scripture comes from 1 Timothy 6:10 (KJV): "For the love of money is the root of all evil: which while some coveted after, they have erred from the faith, and pierced themselves through with many sorrows". The amplified translation re ads: "F or the love of money is a root of all evils: it is through craving that some have been led astray and have wandered from the faith and pierced themselves through with acute (mental) pangs".

We can take any scripture out of context and make any point we want. However, in this text, in his warning against false teachers, Timothy reminds us that if our desire and quest for money takes priority over our faith and love for the things of God, then that desire and quest for money is the root of all evil and brings with it negative consequences.

You see, money is amoral. It is neither good nor bad. However, people can choose to use it to do good things or they can choose to use it to do bad things. It's okay to have money as long as money doesn't have us. Think about it! We all know it takes money to live. It also takes money to advance the Kingdom of God and to help our favorite organizations that bring value to other people's lives. That should be our number one reason for desiring to have money..... money with a mission.....prosperity with purpose.

Psalm 37:5 (KJV) says: "Let them shout for joy, and be glad, that favor my righteous cause: yea, let them say continually, Let the Lord be magnified, which hath pleasure in the prosperity of his people". Yes, God wants us to prosper!

There are over 2,000 scriptures in the Bible about money. In fact, Jesus talked more about money than any other subject. I would say that makes money an important subject, wouldn't you? Money affords us nice things......like nice houses, nice cars, designer clothes, fine jewelry and expensive toys. There's nothing wrong with that as long as our quest to get the money to buy those things doesn't pull us away from the things of God and allows God to remain first place in our lives.

You may be thinking, "I know God wants me to be prosperous in my finances but how do I position myself to do that?"

I'm glad you asked! But first, I have a question for you. What's your financial IQ? What do you know about money? What do you think about money? What are you doing with the money you have? If you need more money what is your plan to get more? The answers to those questions will be based on your core belief system. What were you taught about money when you were growing up? What have you learned as an adult that changed or altered your financial IQ for the better?

When I grew up our family believed in the 40-40 plan. Get a "good" education, go to college and find a job with a "good" company with "good" benefits. Work 40 hours per week and in 40 years you can retire and live a "good" life. Get an education, work hard, pay your bills, save and invest. So, that's what I did. As I approach retirement age, I've definitely learned some things along the way. Financial education and money management are essential if we are to increase our financial portfolio. Becoming financially literate positions us to prosper financially and learning to properly manage money will position us to keep our money.

How sad is it when we hear of professional athletes and movie stars who have earned hundreds of millions of dollars over time and find themselves broke today? It is mind boggling! Poverty and wealth are not just indicators of the amount of money a person possesses. They are states of mind. That is why you could give a homeless person $10,000 to help him/her better their life and if they don't have a clue about financial matters or have the means to find someone who does, they will be penniless and right back on the street in very little time.

People who win the multi-million dollar lottery often find themselves in this same position. In 3-5 years they find themselves right back in the same financial place they started, if not worse. If they had a poverty mentality before and that doesn't change, no amount of money will guarantee sustained wealth because wealth is a mindset and so is poverty.

The 40-40 Plan is an honest way to earn a living, and I'm grateful for what it has afforded me over the years; but it may not be the best way if you want unlimited financial gain, including financial freedom and time freedom. Have you ever heard of the Cash Flow Quadrant? In his book, RICH DAD POOR DAD, Robert Kiyosaki, who is recognized internationally as one of today's leading financial experts, shares this system he learned from his "Rich Dad". It is a diagram that is made of four different people who make up the business world: E stands for Employees, Sstands for Small Businesses, Self-Employed or Specialists like doctors and attorneys, B stands for Big Businesses and I stands for Investors.

On the left side of the quadrant are the E's and S's.

If your core belief system is security you will most likely be an employee with a safe, secure job with benefits. The problem with that in the year 2015 is that the jobs that used to be considered "secure" are no longer "secure". So we need a Plan B, which will be discussed a little later.

If your core belief system says: "I don't want to work for anyone else. I want to be my own boss", you will most likely be a small business owner or self-employed. There is still a sense of security in that you believe you have control over your future. That doesn't give you much leverage though, because you have to do everything yourself.

On the right side of the quadrant are the B's and I's.

The **B's or Big Business Owners are looking for financial freedom and time freedom.** They don't want to run the company by themselves so they seek out good systems, good networks and the smartest people they can find to run it for them.

The fourth part of the quadrant is made up of the I's or Investors. Instead of working hard for their money they learn to make their money work hard for them. Investors are Big Business Owners that invest their excess income in vehicles that are the most profitable and they enjoy the largest legal tax benefits. People in the E and S quadrants often find themselves working hard for the I's.

Depending on your vision, now you can see why the 40-40 Plan may not be the best plan, especially if it's your only plan. Working as an employee will only allow you to go so far. No matter how many times you are promoted you will always hit that proverbial financial ceiling and no matter how hard you work, how many problems you solve or creative ideas you share, you can NEVER own the company.

Maybe you don't want to own the company. Maybe you don't want to own your own business or move from the left side of the quadrant to the right side. That is your choice and there is nothing wrong with that.

However, if you want financial freedom and time freedom you can only find it on the "right" side ----no pun intended.

Maybe you are already operating on the right side of the quadrant and if that is the case then you can definitely validate these principles.

If not, but you are interested in positioning yourself to prosper financially, you will have to begin to change your mind-set to move from the left side of the Cash Flow Quadrant to the right side.

Ladies, we are each fearfully and wonderfully made in the image of God. Each of us has been "tagged". We are unique and we were born with talents, abilities and gifts. We were also created with a divine purpose. Once we discover that divine purpose we are to use our talents, gifts and abilities to serve the world and glorify God. With that in mind, what are you good at that comes naturally and easily to you? What is it that you enjoy doing so much that you would do even if no one paid you to do it? What is it that gives you that deep sense of satisfaction and purpose?

Begin to think of ways to use your talents, gifts and abilities to make you wealthy instead of making others wealthy. Think of ways to serve your gift to the world and accept wealth along the way. As I approach retirement age, realizing that my traditional plan will not be enough, I have already positioned myself on the right side of the Cash Flow Quadrant by having a home-based business. Having been married to an Entrepreneur for nine years, I have been exposed to a different mindset and have had the opportunity to be exposed to several business opportunities until finding the right fit for me. If I'm to be totally honest, it has not been an easy transition….moving from an employee mindset to one of an entrepreneur.

Being an entrepreneur comes with more responsibility and it involves taking a certain amount of calculated risks. We have always been involved with some type of Network Marketing Company and if I've learned one thing it is this: Network Marketing is a SYSTEM that stands for Save Yourself Stress Time Energy and Money.

I am a professional elementary school counselor by trade and I love what I do! It is self-fulfilling and counseling comes naturally to me. I am an educator who is compassionate and loves helping others. I believe that is my calling so as I think about leaving the traditional E quadrant as an employee I am in the process of forming my LLC that will allow me to contract with schools, churches and other organizations to provide specialized programs for children like Sexual Abuse Prevention and Bully Prevention. I will use my talents, gifts, and abilities matched with the training and experience I gained in the corporate world to create my own wealth.

Because I believe in multiple streams of income I will also use my time to continue to build my network marketing businesses to a level that will afford me the financial freedom and time freedom that I desire. My businesses will help fund my dreams and allow me to be a blessing to others.

Why Network Marketing? Read what the experts have to say:

"Network Marketing is The Perfect Business" *for the average person to create wealth." -- Rich Dad Poor Dad by Robert Kiyosaki, Author and Multi-Millionaire*

"If I lost everything and had to start again, I would find myself a great network marketing company and get to work!" *---Donald Trump, Globally Renowned Property Mongul and Multi-Billionaire*

"The Best Investment ever made..." *---Warren Buffet, Billionaire Investor and the Richest Man in the World*

"From 2006 to 2016, there will be 10 Million new Millionaires in the U.S. alone, more than double the last decade....many will be from the Direct Selling Industry!" *–Paul Zane Pilzer, World Renowned Economist and Best-Selling Author*

"If I would be given a chance to start all over again, I would choose NETWORK MARKETING." *--- Bill Gates, Microsoft Chief Software Architect and Multi- Billionaire*

If the "Greats" of the business world endorse Network Marketing as the business vehicle of choice, the question is no longer what kind of business but rather which network marketing company to choose?

There are countless numbers of network marketing companies that offer a plethora of products and services providing you the opportunity to find the right fit for you.

Here are 7 Great Benefits of Network Marketing:

1. Flexibility- You can work virtually from anywhere as long as you have a computer and a phone.
2. Low start-up cost with free comprehensive training
3. Determine your own income and your own future
4. Provides a variety of products and services from which to choose
5. No overhead, No inventory, No employees
6. Opportunities for self-development
7. Excellent tax benefits

Success is based upon helping others to succeed which often develops into friendships and lasting relationships.

Even with all the data to support network marketing as the business of the 21st Century, you might still say it is not for you. That is okay; remember it's your choice. If you're looking for security which, in some cases has become a false sense of security, then remain an employee but work your Plan B. In time, your Plan B just might become your Plan A. Use your talents and gifts to bring increase to yourself. You will be one step closer to making the paradigm shift. Your Plan B may or may not be network marketing. It might be an entrepreneurial business or service business. It could be a landscape business, training, consulting, life coach, health coach, tutoring, painting, writing, crafts, woodworking, computers, photography, or even cooking. What are you passionate about?

Proverbs 4:7 (KJV) says, "Wisdom is the principal thing; therefore get wisdom: and with all thy getting get understanding".

If you are an employee and you desire to become a business owner and investor, it is wise to have an exit plan. It would not be prudent to just up and quit your job without a plan to sustain you until you are making a profit in your business. Jim Rohn, great American entrepreneur, author and motivational speaker said it best, "Work full-time on your job and part-time on your fortune and you will soon be working full-time on your fortune."

If you're looking for financial freedom and time freedom you will have to make the shift to the right side of the Cash Flow Quadrant where profits are better than wages. Wages will make you a living but profits can make you a fortune. (Jim Rohn)

Remember earlier, when I mentioned that the jobs we once considered to be secure are no longer as secure as they once were? Remember when we thought if we worked for the big companies like the US Postal Service, AT&T, Sprint, Delta, UPS, Fed-Ex, Bank of America, or even in Education, we thought we were safe? With massive downsizing, outsourcing and reorganization, that is no longer the case. Well, not only are those jobs no longer as secure as they once were, neither is the value of the American dollar.

You may be thinking, "What does one thing have to do with the other?" Well, we work for money and in 1971 our money stopped being money and became a currency when it ceased being backed by gold. Did you know that Gold is God's money? But that's another story for another time. The value of the US dollar is falling and savers are finding their savings wiped out with very little left for retirement.....except Social Security and Medicare, which are also in trouble. The middle class is dwindling and if this trend continues we will find ourselves in a two-class society---the rich and the poor. If that becomes the case, where do you want to be?

Ninety percent of women will have to manage their finances on their own at some point in their life. ("Women in the Labor Force: A Databook", U.S. Bureau of Statistics, 2012) They may leave the workforce to care for a sick family member, become divorced, or find themselves widowed. Or they may be one of many young adults who are staying single longer and living on their own for longer than past generations. That's why it is imperative for women to have a solid understanding about how to manage money and invest for the future.

Or you may be like the Proverbs 31 Woman who was a wife and a mother. She knew finances and was an Entrepreneur. She was in the real estate business, she had a sewing business and she was a great helpmate to her husband.

Whatever the case, to position yourself to prosper financially you must increase your financial literacy. Here are some helpful tips:

- Find a mentor in the area in which you are interested.
- Read books, magazines and online articles about financial literacy
- Listen to financial literacy CD's and books on tape
- Attend financial literacy seminars
- Join financial organizations
- Watch videos on financial literacy

I would be remiss if I did not mention the fact that there is a natural side to financial prosperity and there is also a spiritual side. The world's system of exchange is buying and selling. However, God's system is sowing and reaping and supersedes the world's system. The most profitable investment you can make is in the Kingdom of God.

Mathew 6:33 (KJV) says, "Seek ye first the kingdom of God and his righteousness; and all these things shall be added unto you". What things...... you know.....stuff...... material things like nice houses, nice cars, designer clothes, fine jewelry and expensive toys or whatever it is that you desire.

In Proverbs 3:9 (KJV) we are instructed to "honor the Lord with... the first fruits of ALL our increase".

Malachi 3:10 (KJV) says, "Bring ye all the tithes into the storehouse, that there may be meat in mine house, and prove me now herewith, saith the Lord of hosts, if I will not open you the windows of heaven and pour you out a blessing, that there shall not be room enough to receive it". God's word is saying that if we bring Him the tithe He will bless us in the overflow.

The tithe is 10% of your income. Giving God 10% and you living off the 90% not only shows that you are in covenant with Him but it also shows God you trust Him. I have seen this principle work in my life for over 30 years now. Sometimes the return is in money and sometimes the return comes in the form of intangibles like God's favor that often translates into money.

Deuteronomy 8:18 (KJV) says, "But thou shalt remember the Lord thy God: for it is he that giveth thee power to get wealth, that he may establish his covenant". Without God, we wouldn't be who we are, be able to do what we do, nor have what we have. So let's not forget our true source.

As you position yourself to prosper, remember there is a natural side and a spiritual side to prosperity. Obedience to God's spiritual laws will cause abundance to manifest in the natural realm. Keep God first and He will bring increase to every area of your life, including your finances. Keep God first and you will truly be Positioned 2 Prosper!

Brenda Stroman

Brenda Stroman is a native of Hampton, Virginia. She graduated from Virginia State University where she earned a B.S. degree in Health, Physical Education and Recreation. Brenda also lived in the Nation's Capital for two and a half years, where she worked for the now rebirthed Eastern Airlines.

After moving to Atlanta in 1982, she continued to work for Eastern until the Labor Strike in 1990.

Being without a job, Brenda relied on her faith in God to sustain her and often refers to that testimony in times of trials and the testing of her faith. She continues to hold onto a famous quote that got her through those unpredictable times, "When you've nothing left but God….God is enough".

After the reorganization of the Airline, she hired on with Atlanta Public Schools where she taught elementary Physical Education for eight and a half years. She returned to school to earn a M.S in Community Counseling with an add-on certificate in School Counseling.

Brenda has been an elementary school counselor for the past 18 years, which is a testament to her love for children.

Brenda attends The Body of Christ Church International, USA where she has been an active member for 28 years. She attributes the successes in her life to the grace of her Lord and Savior, Jesus Christ.

The Godly seed planted by her beloved grandmother when she was a child laid a solid foundation for the sound biblical principles she has learned through personal and corporate bible study and the uncompromised Word of God taught by her spiritual father and mother, Drs. Joseph and Marjanita Ripley.

Throughout her membership at The Body of Christ, Brenda has served in the Maintenance, Audio Visual, Teen Ministry, Counseling, and Music Departments and presently serves as a Greeter in the Hospitality Department.

She and her husband Anthony shared the responsibility of coordinating Business by the Book, an outreach ministry for part- time and full-time business owners, based on biblical principles.

Brenda is an avid reader and researcher. Over the years, she has attended numerous financial, business and personal development conferences and workshops. Having worked alongside her husband Anthony, whose mission is to teach others how to eradicate debt and poor health and create generational wealth, she has accumulated a wealth of knowledge, which she has so eloquently shared in this chapter of Positioned 2 Prosper.

In her spare time, Brenda built two home-based network marketing business.....one in the Health and Wellness Industry and the other, teaching others how to diversify their savings in Gold, God's money.

For more information:

Anthony Stroman
Zooma.com/healing
678.907.3135
"Improving Your Health and Creating Wealth"

CHAPTER SEVEN

~

Be Made Whole Health and Wellness

Evangelist Patsy Cole, CBT

Health and Wellness

One of the most profound truths concerning the human race is located on the sacred pages of the Bible. It declares, *"My people perish for the lack of knowledge."* One might present an argument as to what audience of people was being referenced in this passage; nonetheless we can agree that everyone lacks knowledge in some area.

As it relates to prosperity, it's evident that our worldview is distorted and many are in a state of ignorance. In the past, I too had misconceptions associated with this word "*prosperous*". Solomon the Great tells us, "*In all your getting-get an understanding.*" The golden nuggets of truth found in each chapter are intended to educate, empower and equip you with tools for building a life of prosperity.

Most women crave to become prosperous. If you are "*that*" woman, I have *Good News!* Your craving can be satisfied today by applying each principle throughout this book. I will begin by dispelling a myth concerning prosperity.

Prosperity Defined

What then is prosperity? The definition is complex, but its meaning is quite simple: It *is to become strong and flourishing,* to become successful and thrive. Although it encompasses wealth, it is not limited to financial and material possessions. It involves factors such as health and happiness. According to Strong's Complete Concordance of the Bible, one Hebrew word for prosperity is shalom

- "*completeness, soundness, welfare and peace.*"

Health Defined

The nuggets shared in this chapter will explore the topic of Health. In short, health is defined as freedom from physical pain. At times it is viewed as merely the absence of disease or infirmity. In a broader sense of the word, health is the condition of being sound in *spirit, soul* and *body*. It is a state of well being – perfection and completeness.

The Health Proclamation

Contrary to popular belief, God took a stand on prosperity as seen in Jeremiah 9: 11 - *"For I know the plans I have for you"*, declares the LORD, *"plans to prosper you and not to harm you, plans to give you hope and a future."* It's His desire that we prosper in every area of our life. 3 John 1:2 confirms this by stating,

"Beloved, I wish above all things that you may prosper and be in health, even as your soul prospers." We will take a closer look at the relationship between the state of our health and the prosperity of our soul later in this chapter.

The Curse – The Cause

In order for us to prosper in health, it's vitally important to first understand the origin of disease. Sickness and disease in any form was never a part of God's plan for man. Disease (*broken ease*) is the direct curse God placed on Earth in result of man's sin. The curse was not limited to our physical body only, but its consequences adversely affected the spirit and soul as well. This downward spiral slowly took man from a state of perfect health to experiencing a widespread of health conditions: *Mental disorders, infectious disease, social depravity* and ultimately death. However, in spite of mans poor choices, God in His mercy created our human bodies with the amazing ability to combat sickness and disease. We should never ignore or take this for granted.

The Redemption – The Purchase

When Jesus died on the cross and rose again, the power of the curse was broken. *"Surely He has borne our grief's and carried our sorrows; yet we esteemed Him stricken, smitten by God, and afflicted. But He was wounded for our transgressions, He was bruised for our iniquities; the chastisement for our peace was upon Him, and by His stripes we are healed."*

Isaiah 53:4-5 does not indicate that our physical bodies will not experience sickness and disease, however it is clear that we the atonement granted us access to healing.

God's thoughts concerning your peace and prosperity are much higher than you could imagine. His desire is to bless and prosper us, give you favor and grace even as it relates to our health. Prepare yourself and put on your imaginary gear! It's time to take an exploration into the deep mines of Health Prosperity. Like any miner, you're sure to come out with treasures of gold that could change your life forever!

Glimpse of the Past

As an adolescent, it was as if the twins Sickness and Disease were issued a restraining order to *"stay away from my body"*. I simply can't recall being sick! How did I manage to complete nine months of school year after year without ever missing a day? Was it those green leafy vegetables I was instructed to eat as a child? – Was it the 9 o'clock weekly curfew, which granted my body plenty of rest? Was I *simply* motivated by the sound of my name being called for Perfect Attendance during the Annual Award Ceremony? Whatever the contributing factor was, I was definitely a benefactor.

Is it true that *"All good things come to an end?"* Excuse me as I push the fast forward button in attempt to answer this question.

BODY - Physical

The Great Attack

I find it interesting that some of the greatest medical discoveries were by means of experimentation or lab testing. Although a Health

Educator, most of the health nuggets I discovered were findings from an involuntary search. It was the health challenges experienced that prompted extended research on Health and Wellness.

In 1996, I felt as if my body was in a war zone. – I was convinced that I would soon become a casualty. There was extreme soreness developing in almost every area of my body. My daily routine was slowly interrupted by the frustration that comes with physical ailments. I remember very well when the aches began. My body was trying to translate a message that something was terribly wrong. However, it was much easier for me to ignore the signs than to schedule a Dr.'s appointment. I could no longer endure. - The pain was shouting "Attention" and I obeyed the command.

Prior to these symptoms occurring, I was considered a very healthy individual. I couldn't imagine what was causing all the discomfort. I spent hours reading medical books hoping to self-diagnose my condition. My efforts were in vain as my pain level continued to increase. The day came when I decided to consult medical help. Two months later, after undergoing several tests, it was as if I had an acting role as the "*Woman with the Issue of Blood*". My financial resources were the condition had grown worse.

The Report

It's been said, "*If Health is a blessing – Sickness is a Curse*". I wasn't quite sure who the guilty culprit was, but I felt like Satan was at least an accomplice. The more I cried and prayed, the more I was reminded of God's promises, *"Weeping might endure for a moment but joy comes in the morning".* – *"By my stripes you are healed."* If only that truth could have manifested in my body. After four months of suffering, I received a medical report disclosing the cause of my pain.

The diagnosis was "fibromyalgia". My physician was very thorough when explaining the details in his report, but the only two words resounding in my spirit were, *"No Cure"*!

The Facts

Even as a Health Professional I was unfamiliar with the facts. According to the national Fibromyalgia Association, this chronic pain disorder affects an estimated 10 million people in the United States. - I happened to be one of the 10 million. The medications prescribed took a toll on my body, weakening my immune system even more. The symptoms associated with this *"uninvited guest"* affected every muscle of my body. I often experienced: *sleep disorders, anxiety, migraines, irritable bowel syndrome, chronic pain*, and *fatigue.*

SOUL – Mind Will & Emotions

The Battlefield

I wish I could have remained strong and full of faith, however, doubt and fear dominated my thoughts. The declining of my health impacted my ability to work. Consequently, I was placed on short- term and later long-term disability. Sadly, The duties as a single parent of four had become too much to handle and I required the assistance of others. My children had to relocate to living with their father and one of my friends.

There comes a moment in the midst of crisis when you feel like giving up. This was one of those times. I had isolated myself from the outside world and went into a state of depression. My energy was depleted; I desperately wanted to be healed. During a period of two years, I experienced so many losses: health*, employment, parent guardianship, property, and social status. –* I *almost* lost my mind!

SPIRIT – Inner Man

The War is Won

Treating the symptoms only will not cure a medical condition or disorder. It's always helpful to find out the underlining cause. "*The truth is in the root.*" After *seemly* exhausting all options, my first plan of action, (*which I abandoned*), had now become my last plan of action. – Seeking, trusting and obeying God. During my Bible study, I was inspired to read the following verse referenced in two different passages "... *The leaves of the tree were for the healing of the nations...* " Rev. 22:2 and Ezekiel 47:12 I interpreted the "leaves" as bringing healing due to their healing properties. Thus, I began my research on herbal supplements and its health benefits. My findings ignited a fire inside of me! I KNEW I was being directed by the Holy Spirit and on a pathway to healing!

I committed myself to a healthy diet and exercise program. The daily intake of herbal products designed to reduce inflammation and strengthen the immune system were being very effective. I escaped that prison of darkness that isolated me from the outside world then resumed to attending weekly worship service. Prayer and fasting had contributed greatly toward the progression of my overall health. Finally, after losing many health battles, the day I long waited for had arrived! I was more than healed! My Spirit was revived! – My Soul rejoiced" – My Body was restored! I was made WHOLE!

The Health Transition

Getting Personal

Health battles have a way of producing good fruit if you provide them spiritual nourishment along the way. Those two years of suffering in my body were life changing. They caused a transformation to take place in my *spirit*, *soul* and *body*. After winning the attack on my body, which was designed to destroy me, my first goal was to obtain optimum health.

Establishing the Problem

I didn't require a medical check-up in order to identify the areas of health that needed maintenance the most. – A few of them were obvious! I was ready to change my status of "obesity". That sounds like a big word because it is. – Obesity is one of the America's leading causes of sickness and disease. As women, we like to think of ourselves as more than a dress size, and I totally agree they we should. However, I realized that my "*dress size*" had caused me way too many health problems than I was willing to accept. Therefore, I began my weight-loss journey.

I was interested in a weight-loss program where the primary focus was not just losing inches and pounds but on one's overall health. I was successful in my search and began a 12-week support class. I learned that it was important to detox your body prior starting any weight-management program. Interestingly, I had to detox my mind first! - Those toxic thoughts such as, "You are going to fail!" were already there to discourage me. I replace those toxic thoughts with, *"I can do ALL things through Christ who gives me strength."* I was now prepared and *positioned to prosper!* The 7-day detox, which included nothing but fruits, vegetables, water and green tea, was amazing! My energy level was off the charts and my mental clarity improved drastically. I was excited and looking forward to *Becoming a Healthier Me!*

Positive Results – Motivators

As a woman desiring to prosper, you will discover many roadblocks on your journey. The most common place where you'll find them set up are in the corners of your mind. As a Christian, I was able to use the authority given to me to *bring negative thoughts into captivity* and *"pull down every stronghold"* used to stop by progress. You too must develop a warrior mentality if you want to prosper. *Satan came to steal kill and destroy our* health. It's up to us to possess it and protect it!

After completing the 12-week program, I reached my short-term goal. – I lost a total of 26lbs. – it wasn't necessary to record the inches, the great loss was obvious! That *dreaded dress size* had changed. I felt good and believed I *looked good!* I was even healed from GERD (R and Alopecia. The positive results motivated me to continue on my health journey. I later became a Certified Transition Lifestyle System Coach. I didn't just stop there. I developed an interest to assist others in times of crisis where counseling would be recommended. I also became certified as a Therapon Belief Therapist. – A Faith-based program promoting Health and Wellness.

The Health Factor

I hope by now you're prepared to achieve some personal wellness goals. Every woman can find at least one area of health where she needs improvement. Those goals might consist of health prevention, weight management, enhancing personal relationships or as simple as learning relaxation techniques. Jesus asked a man, "Do you want to be made whole?" For someone whose health condition had affected his quality of life, I would say that was a pertinent question. Procrastination is said to be *"a thief of time"*, therefore the best time to start toward your health goals is NOW!

Nuggets to Live By

Spiritual Wellness

The Spirit is the innermost being of man. This area is of utmost importance as you get in a *position to prosper*. The Holy Spirit in us enables us to have victory over the war within and the *war without*.

However, we must still nourish our spirit on a daily basis. A person who has an un-nourished spirit will definitely *fulfill the lust of the flesh*. - That's NOT indicative of a prosperous woman!

- **Spiritual Food**
- Prayer
- Meditation
- Worship
- Bible Study
- Serving

Inspirational Nuggets

"I say, walk by the Spirit, and you will not gratify the desires of the flesh."

Galatians 5:16

"For those who are according to the flesh set their minds on the things of the flesh, but those who are according to the Spirit, the things of the Spirit. For the mind set on the flesh is death, but the mind set on the Spirit is life and peace."

He who has an ear let him hear what the Spirit says to the churches to him who overcomes, I will grant to eat of the tree of life which is in the Paradise of God."

Revelation 2:7

"Let no corrupting talk come out of your mouths, but only such as is good for building up, as fits the occasion, that it may give grace to those who hear. And do not grieve the Holy Spirit of God, by whom you were sealed for the day of redemption."

Ephesians 4:29-30

Mental/Emotional Wellness - Overall Psychological Well-being

Stress – Stress is normal and almost impossible to avoid. If not handled properly, it can resort to chronic stress. This type of stress will have negative effects on the body and the mind. Its been medically proven that women deal with stress in a healthier manner than men. Nonetheless, there are still a small group of women who lack healthy stress skills.

Stress Triggers

- Illness
- Divorce
- Death
- Pregnancy
- Holidays
- Retirement

Stress Relief

1. <u>Exercise/Physical Activity</u> – Improves your mood. Consider walking, jogging, swimming, biking. – Anything that will keep you active.
2. <u>Connections</u> – Cultivating friendships with family and friends. It provides a support system. Volunteer for a charitable group.
3. <u>Laughter</u> – Lightens your mental load. Attend a comedy show.
4. <u>Mental Stimulation</u> – Sharpen the brain by reading a book. Play mind games. (Trivia) Complete a crossword puzzle.

Inspirational Nuggets

"We demolish arguments and every pretension that sets itself up against the knowledge of God, and we take captive every thought to make it obedient to Christ."
2 Corinthians 10:5

"Wherefore lay apart all filthiness and superfluity of naughtiness, and receive with meekness the engrafted word, which is able to save your souls."
James 1:21

"Finally, brothers, whatever is true, whatever is honorable, whatever is just, whatever is pure, whatever is lovely, whatever is commendable, if there is any excellence, if there is anything worthy of praise, think about these things."
Philippians 4:8

"Do not be conformed to this world, but be transformed by the renewal of your mind, that by testing you may discern what is the will of God, what is good and acceptable and perfect will of God."

Romans 12:2

Physical Wellness – Total Health of the Body

Our wellness approach should not be just to avoid sickness and disease. We should be concerned about our physical fitness as well as our physical appearance. Should invest our time and resources toward anything that will benefit our total health.

Physical Maintenance

1. Drink water
2. Get plenty of rest
3. Build your immune system / Take Multi-vitamins/ Supplementation
4. Daily Exercise – Movement
5. Daily allowance of fruits & vegetables
6. Schedule Annual Check-ups
7. Quarterly Detox

Hot Topic: Menopause

This is a natural occurrence in a woman's body. It causes some women to worry, which often lead to other health problems. The effects it has on women and its symptoms vary from person to person. Although this stage of The following is my prayer and desire for you, as you become the prosperous woman you were created to be. Once you believe in God – Believe in yourself – You will then be in the perfect "*Position to Prosper*".

"Now may the God of peace himself sanctify you completely, and may your whole spirit and soul and body be kept blameless at the coming of our Lord Jesus Christ."

1 Thessalonians 5:23

ABOUT PATSY CROSS-COLE

Founder & CEO – Be Made Whole Ministries

*Licensed Minister*Professional Educator*Certified Health & Wellness Coach*Author Public Speaker*Mentor* Entrepreneur*Certified Belief Therapist

Live…Love…Laugh is not just her motto, Patsy emulates this on a daily basis. As a blessed wife and mother of 5, she intentionally embraces each God-given day by displaying charity and expressing joy to all those she encounters. It has always been her heart's desire to help people and to make a difference in the lives of others. As an advocate for the disadvantaged, she realizes that all people are important and everyone has the potential for greatness.

Although Patsy received salvation at a young age, she discovered the intentions of God for her life in 1998, and accepted the ministry call to "Do the work of an Evangelist". She serves on the Ministerial Team and Outreach Ministry at Koinonia Christian Church in Arlington, TX. under the Leadership of Dr. Ronnie Goines. Due to her hidden, yet traumatic past of childhood molestation, FEAR continued the attempt to sabotage her destiny. However, in 2006, Patsy defeated the odds and became the Founder of Be Made Whole Ministries, which focuses on holistic healing of the spirit, soul and body. Its mere existence is to empower, encourage and equip others to move beyond their painful past and present challenges into a purpose-driven life. Her Be Made Whole Center Unfranchise Business is a compliment to her ministry. As a survivor of divorce, single parenthood, health challenges (Fibromyalgia) and molestation, Patsy understands what it means to overcome challenges prevalent in today's society. She longs to see others transformed from feelings of inadequacy and insignificance to lives of confidence and influence.

A sought after conference speaker, Patsy takes the hope and healing message to religious and secular audiences. Her passionate delivery and transparent heart, captivates and delights people of all ages, genders and backgrounds. Each message is rich with scripture, real life stories, candor, practical steps and relevant analogies. Her presentations shine with clarity and engaging examples while stirring the heart of those who seek emotional and spiritual freedom. Patsy's article entitled "Sharing My Story", has been published in Run On Magazine. She has appeared as guest on: Joshua Generation Radio, Radio Therapy with Terrance J., Breaking of Bread Radio Talk Show, LA Talk Radios Heart of Soul and 6th Man Production "Getting to Know" Series. Patsy was honored as a "Survivor" by Women with Gifts, at the 2015 "I Survived Gospel Concert".

She holds fast to the truth that people are able to conquer any adversity they may face. As a Mentor, Patsy's compelling passion for women's ministry and to help hurting humanity is ever- increasing. She hosted Meet Me in the Spirit Women's Conference in 2007-2008 and Reveal Your Glory Women's Gathering in 2015. Patsy holds a Bachelor of Science Degree majoring in Health and Physical Education, a member of Delta Sigma Theta Sorority and a recipientof Who's Whoamong Studentsin Collegesand Universities. She recently ended a 18 year career as a Middle School Christian Educator. As Co-Author of "Phenomenal, That's Me", her endeavor is to inspire readers to discover the pathway to freedom and wholeness. Patsy is also excited about the curriculum development and publication to be used during her Free to Be Free Workshops launching in 2016!

Without a doubt, this earthen vessel has truly had an encounter with God. In result, He has released upon her a fresh prophetic and healing anointing. As God continues to build His character in her, Patsy is truly learning what it means to go from faith to faith and from glory to glory.

"I don't want notoriety; my desire is for my life to be a reflection of what I believe. My greatest desire with the exception of household salvation, is to reach the masses with the saving knowledge of Jesus Christ by any means necessary and to see people "Free for Real"! I've had many giants to contend with, however, God has not allowed me to be overthrown by any of them. Yes, I've been crushed...BUT... without the crushing of the olive, there is NO oil!"

Past and Current Platforms:

*Prisons*Emergency Shelters*Empowerment Workshops*Worship
Services
*Radio Stations*Hospitals*Senior Centers*Magazine
Publication*Newsletter Articles
*Health & Wellness Fairs*Symposium Panel*Community Outreach
Events

CHAPTER EIGHT

❧

Prosperous Marriage

Pastor Tara L. Alexander

Prosperous Marriage

After close to 30 years of marriage I was asked to share on a subject that is very dear to my heart and that is Marriage and Prosperity in Marriage. So in doing so, I want to share some of my life experiences that lead me to this God ordained union. I will also be equipping you with some of my favorite scriptures that I personally have stood on in my search of what I believe was designed to be one of the most healthiest relationships outside of that between me and my heavenly Father and that is marriage. Before I do that I would like to share a very brief history about me. Well for starters, my parents were divorced when I was very young so there was never a fulltime male figure in my life, so growing up I never saw what I would consider a healthy marriage. The marriages that I encountered were not healthy or stable marriages. Even though I, along with my siblings were brought up in a church environment (religion) I could still pick up on what seemed to be pure unhappiness even in the wives of church goers. At a very young age I would see the lies, the cheating the fighting, the unhappiness, belittling of the wives and even the manipulation of and by the wives. I remember as a young child thinking to myself if this is what marriage is like; I don't want any part of this.

As I grew my desire to be married changed from not wanting to be married to maybe one day I will get married. But guess what, even though I wanted no part of marriage as a young child there were still some of those warped traits I picked up and opinions that I formed that did not truly surface until I was married.

Once married it was as if two worlds had collided and I needed to learn how to really be married and apply all I had learned good and bad. I needed to stand my ground. I needed to show that I was a religious wife. It was only through much prayer and acknowledging that I needed help and discipline that I was able to overcome the obstacles that were designed to destroy my marriage, and religion was the main thing.

When I look at all that I went through it still amazes me that God had a purpose for me and saw fit to bless me with a prosperous marriage and the opportunity to work with so many wonderful couples. At times when I speak with couples all I can say is but God. You see what the enemy thought he could use to destroy my perception and taint my view, God turned it around and not only blessed me with an amazing husband but set me on the path to a prosperous marriage. Through it all he has equipped my husband and I with the tools needed to help others enjoy a healthy, happy marriage.

Notice I said earlier that I was brought up in a church environment (religion) so I learned all the gestures when to smile and how to play the role. I also learned how to submit even with hatred in my heart, because this is some of what I grew up around.

I would like to share a few key points that I believe positioned me to prosper in the area of marriage.

Forgiveness

I had to learn to forgive my father and all the people that I felt had disappointed me. Forgiveness was the key that unlocked the prison that I willfully went to frequently.

Mark 11: 25-26 *And when ye stand praying, forgive, if ye have ought against any: that your father which is also in heaven may forgive you your trespasses. But if ye do not forgive, neither will your father which is in heaven forgive your trespasses.*

Matthew 6:14 *For if you forgive men their trespasses, your heavenly Father will also forgive you.*

Prayer

I had to start spending time in prayer for me because I knew there were some things in me that needed to be dealt with. As right as I tried to make my wrong, only in prayer could I see my true reality who I was really designed to be.

Matthew 21:22 *And in all things, whatsoever Ye shall ask in prayer, believing ye shall receive.*

Develop my personal healthy relationship with my heavenly father and learn that he wanted the best for me all along.

Proverbs 3:5 *trust in the lord with all your heart and lean not to your own understanding but in all your ways acknowledge him and he shall direct your path.*

3 John 2 *Beloved I wish above all things that thou may prosper and be in health even as your soul prospers.*

I had to be open to position myself around healthy relationships. One of the hardest things I had to do was to learn the difference between religion and relationship.

The Bible instructs us in ***Proverbs 4:7*** wisdom is the principle thing *therefore get wisdom and in all thy getting get understanding* I decide to go on a personal journey to seek the truth about marriage. While seeking the truth I realized the importance of a few key points that lead to a healthy marriage.

- Pray about everything
- Understand who created marriage
- Understand the purpose of marriage
- Understand that marriage is a gift
- Understand that people are human
- Understand that marriage takes work
- Understand prosperity in a marriage means more than finances
- Purpose of finances

All of this was necessary for me in order for me to truly walk in what I was purposed for. I had to learn who I was in God. I had to understand that God created me. I also had to learn to love myself.

As I endeavored on my search for truth about marriage, I finally realized that marriage was created by God and not by man. It was at that moment that I realized and had a clear understanding that when God created marriage it was intended to be a lifelong commitment until death do us part. I also had to learn that marriage was just not to make me happy but that it was designed with a purpose in mind and that any and everything about my marriage should bring glory to God and therefore have no place for selfishness. And last but not least that marriage is a Gift that we choose to accept.

Now imagine all that I went through and now I am entering into a marriage set in my ways but knowing deep down inside that there had to be something different and better to a marriage. Knowing that what I had seen in church and on television at a young age was not the real representation of what God intended for marriage.

My mission became to shed everything that I thought my little mind knew of marriage and to learn how to do it God's way. In doing so I found that the identity I had was a counterfeit I picked up in order to protect me from the pain I grew up around. When I really started to get an understanding of God and his purpose for me and my marriage it was a reality check because God was so patient with me in my unlearning process he taught me his way in comparison to the worlds way of marriage. For a time I had to separate myself just long enough for him to equip me to go back into the environment that I was brought up in with love and understanding.

One of the most important lessons I have learned about marriage is that people can only give you what they have or what they have been exposed to. In other words if no one around you has or have had a healthy marriage then how can they teach you about a having healthy marriage. It is one thing to talk about a healthy marriage and another thing to walk in it or be a living example of the manifestations a healthy marriage.

Hard times are going to come to those who get married. Hard times are going to come to your soul. Your Mind, Will, Emotions, Intellect and Imagination.

Your **mind** - how you process things. But you have to remember;

Romans 12:2 - *And be not conformed to this world: but be ye transformed by the **renewing of your mind**, that ye may prove what [is] that good, and acceptable, and perfect, will of God.*

2 Corinthians 10:5 - *Casting down imaginations, and every high thing that exalteth itself against the knowledge of God, and bringing into captivity every thought to the obedience of Christ;*

Isaiah 26:3 - *Thou wilt keep [him] in perfect peace, [whose] mind [is] stayed [on thee]: because he trusteth in thee.*

Your **will** the way you want to do things. But the word of God tells us in **Philippians 2:13** - *For it is God which worketh in you both to will and to do of [his] good pleasure.*

Matthew 6:33-34 - *But seek ye first the kingdom of God, and his righteousness; and all these things shall be added unto you.*

Your emotions - the way you process things. You have to practice being a character driven individual and not an emotional driven person. **Proverbs 29:11** - *A fool uttereth all his mind: but a wise [man] keepeth it in till afterwards.*

Proverbs 15:18 - *A wrathful man stirreth up strife: but [he that is] slow to anger appeaseth strife.*

Galatians 5:16-24 - *[This] I say then, Walk in the Spirit, and ye shall not fulfil the lust of the flesh.*

Your **Intellect** - how you think things should be processed with your knowledge. This particular passage says it all,

John 14:6 - *Jesus saith unto him, I am the way, the truth, and the life: no man cometh unto the Father, but by me.*

Learn to change your confession

In order to learn to change my confession I had to learn what God said about a wife, a husband and marriage. I had to start saying that. Confessing what the word of God says and not what I saw or what I believed.

I had to learn that my words were seeds and what I spoke or what I wanted had to line up with what God was saying, when he said what he said.

We have to go back to coming to God with child- like faith that faith that says; **Matthew 19:26** *nothing is impossible with God and with him all things are possible.*

One thing I would like to share with anyone desiring to get married is to do your research study yourself, study your family and do the same with the person you are marrying. Ask questions, talk about everything, and get an understanding about where you both stand on certain topics.

Communication - *learn how to talk to one another not at one another.*

Finances - *learn who is stronger when it comes to handling finances and the purpose of finances.*

Religion - *learn about your future spouse's beliefs.*

Family/Children - *talk about having and raising children.*

Sex - *talk about sexual concerns and beliefs.*

Divorce - *talk about your beliefs concerning divorce.*

Goals - *set short term and long term goals.*

I would say communicate, communicate, communicate it has been said that communication is one of the main reasons for divorce so with that being said communicate.

Jeremiah 29:11 For I know the plans I have for you," declares the Lord, "plans to prosper you and not to harm you, plans to give you hope and a future.

Amos 3:3 How can two walk together unless they agree.

Pastor Steve and Tara Alexander
Covenant Couples Ministry, OKC

When I think about prosperity in a marriage I am reminded of one of my favorite scriptures, *3 John 2 (AMP)* 2 Beloved, I pray that in every way you may succeed and prosper and be in good health [physically], just as [I know] your soul prospers [spiritually]

Prosperity

Most people, when they hear prosperity, they connect it to money or finances only. So even if everything else is going good in your marriage or relationships most will not see that as prosperity, But I believe when the scripture says prosperity, it is talking about every area of your life balancing which would then include money and finances. I believe that God wants our mind, will and emotions to be in a healthy mode so that we can enjoy the finances. Imagine being sick physically or mentally then what good would money be to you. I believe that God wants us to prosper at everything we do, he wants us to have knowledge and understanding going into our different situations because if not what are the chances that we will do the same thing that Adam did in the garden and point the figure and shift the blame and say we did not know.

Sometimes we settle and accept less than what God has for us but God wants you and I to be successful and to have the best of whatever he blesses us with but we have to know this about our heavenly father, if not we will just go through life just settling for any and everything; never really seeking out the best. I had to learn this the hard way. I had to learn how to ask, how to seek, and how to knock and then really trust that God was looking out for my good.

Hosea 4:6 (AMP) My people are destroyed because they have not learned. You were not willing to learn. So I am not willing to have you be My religious leader. Since you have forgotten the Law of your God, I also will forget your children.

James 4:3 You ask and do not receive, because you ask amiss, that you may spend it on your pleasures.

What is God's purpose for marriage?

Genesis 2:18 Amplified Bible (AMP)

18 Now the Lord God said, "It is not good (beneficial) for the man to be alone; I will make him a helper [one who balances him a counterpart who is] suitable and complementary for him.

Genesis 2:24 Amplified Bible (AMP)

For this reason a man shall leave his father and his mother, and shall be joined to his wife; and they shall become one flesh.

- Prosperity successful flourishing thriving condition prosperous circumstance
- It has always been God's desire for us to prosper
- Prosperity in a marriage exemplifies healthiness
- Attributes of a prosperous marriage
- Keys that lead to a healthy marriage
- Prayer
- Understand who created marriage
- Understand the purpose of marriage
- Understand marriage is a gift
- Understand roles in a marriage

I feel prayer is so important in our marriages because the more time we spend in prayer the more our wants and desires change to what God wants for our lives. The more we seek God the more he will allow us to be exposed to the purpose of our desires and wants. I remember early in our marriage always praying that God would use our marriage as an instrument to bring him glory I did not just want a typical marriage but I wanted people to know that without a shadow of doubt in my mind that it was all God, because if it had solely been on us we would have walked away years ago. I cannot stress enough the power in prayer because so many times we want to take credit for what God has and is still doing in our marriage.

- Allow God to change your perception of marriage
- Get God's view on marriage
- Read the word
- Get God's view on marriage
- Study the word
- Meditate on the word
- Change your declaration

As a wife, this is what I've found in my private time of seeking the Lord on how to have the mind of Christ. As a wife, how to love as a godly woman and how to serve my husband. These are the nuggets that were revealed to me and I hope you are blessed with them as well.

1. Don't publicly criticize or correct your spouse remember they are not the children.

2. It is as simple as this! If you don't consider your spouse somebody else will.

3. I absolutely love my husband, there is no greater feeling than knowing you are loved and appreciated by those you are in covenant with. He hears me even when I don't speak. I thank God for my praying Priest.

4. Ask God to teach you how to pray for your spouse not prey on someone else's spouse.

5. Be careful who you whisper your secrets to.

6. Married couples be careful who you vent to about what your spouses are doing and not doing because while you Are venting there are some taking notes for personal gain.

7. All of us would love to have a perfect marriage but is it such a thing? I have yet to see one. All marriages, let me say that again, all marriages require work, sacrifices and compromise. The question is are you willing to work and sacrifice and compromise for yours?

Last but not least I would like to close with a prayer;

Father God your word says that if any of us lack wisdom to ask. Father we come to you in the name of your son Jesus Christ asking you to heal and restore those broken marriages. Father teach us to prosper in our marriages as our souls prosper according to your written and known word. Father we ask you to direct our paths to a place of learning. Renew our love and our relationships with you. Teach us to hear what the spirit of the Lord is saying pertaining to prosperity in marriages. Let us be a light that shines ever so bright directing people to you. These and all things we ask in your son Jesus' name Amen.

Covenant Couples

ABOUT PASTOR TARA ALEXANDER

Pastor Tara Alexander has a heart for hurting women. This passion and fire that burns inside of her was fueled after a spiritual attack on her marriage many years ago. Not having a spiritual mother or mentor, and not having an understanding of the importance of surrounding yourself with a Godly support system, caused Pastor Tara to now demonstrate the love and uncompromising compassion toward marriage, ministry and God's daughters. Through this love, she is affectionally known as "Mama T."

After the spiritual attack on her marriage, Pastor Tara conducted a genealogical study of divorce in her and her husband's family and noted its significance. Understanding that she and her husband, Pastor Steve Alexander, who have been married for 30 years, withstood the enemy's assault on their marriage, she realized the magnitude of the war that the enemy had for God's marriage covenant and its symbolic position in ministry and in life.

In 1995 Pastor Tara Alexander and her husband founded Covenant Couples Family Ministries in Oklahoma City. Their mission is to develop healthy productive marriages to advance God's kingdom on earth by teaching, ministering and counseling on the biblical truth of a God ordained marriage as well as expose the enemy and his tactics used to destroy the institute of marriages thus empower and encourage couples to stay in the battle and fight for the covenant they made with one another. The other areas that God has anointed Pastor Tara and her husband in is the area of ministering to singles, singles seeking marital relationship, as well as financial stewardship in the body of Christ. In addition to their personal ministry, they support and work alongside other Christian organizations with leadership. Developing programs and workshops, helping and encouraging leaders to develop and maintain spiritually healthy and balanced lifestyle.

Working in the field of dentistry for over 30 years as an office manager Pastor Tara has ensured the care of giving back to the community, by support organizations such as Walk Against Breast Cancer, Out of Darkness Walk Against Suicide Prevention, Salvation Army Food Drives, and Mission of Mercy-Free Dental Care. Pastor Tara along with her husband, both individually as well as together, has been the guest speaker at many different marriage conferences, workshops locally and nationally as well as several appearances on TBN.

One of Pastor Tara's many goals as an ambassador of God's kingdom is to help women who may not fully understand how unique and powerful they are as described in Proverbs 31. Her teaching inspires and challenges women to develop a strong relationship with God and with their families. She is an anointed preacher and teacher of the word of God and her message is straightforward and always encouraging others to walk strongly in the purpose into which God has called you.

CHAPTER NINE

∽

Emotions

Master your emotions, master your life.

Emotion is created by motion

Whatever you focus on, you feel.

Happiness is a choice. And so is depression, anger, frustration, or any other emotion.

Don't be ruled by your emotions ...they will derail your problem solving.
Respond appropriately by choosing to act in faith not fear.
- Dr. I.V Hilliard

The truth is, you can feel any emotion you want by DECIDING to feel it.

No one makes you feel "happy" or "angry", **it's based on how you're interpreting each situation in your life and the meaning you associate to it.**

Everybody has emotions. They are a part of who God made us to be and a part of our spiritual makeup. It is important that we acknowledge our emotions and learn how to align them with the Word of God.

God has given us authority over everything in the earth, including our emotions.

Emotions are "feelings caused by pain or pleasure that try to move you in a certain direction."

Women verbalize, while men internalize.

If your emotions are in charge of your life, they will determine the direction of your life. When you are in charge of your life and the Word is your final authority, your emotions will line up with God and His Word.

Emotions are part of the soulish realm.

3 John 2:2

2 Beloved, I pray that you may prosper in all things and be in health, just as your soul prospers.

God created us to dominate; however, we were not designed to dominate people. People who try to control others don't have control over their own emotions.

Mastering your emotions doesn't mean that you can no longer express them.

God designed us to express passion and emotions.

Controlling your emotions;

You must not be ruled by your emotions as they can constantly change.

Emotions are designed to take you somewhere. Ask yourself: *Where are my emotions taking me?*

It is important that you allow the Word of God to control your emotions and decisions.

When your thoughts line up with the Word, your emotions will fall in line, and you will have peace and security.

If you can control your emotions, you can do anything.

Proverbs 16:32 says that a person who can control his emotions is more powerful than an army that can take a city.

Golden Nuggets:

- You can take control over your emotions
- Self-control is a godly force that God uses to direct your life where He has designed it to go.
- Uncontrolled or unyielding emotions lead to confusion and chaos in ones life.

Jesus had emotions but His emotions did not have control over Him. Hebrews 4:15

15 For we have not an high priest which cannot be touched with the feeling of our infirmities; but was in all points tempted like as we are, yet without sin.

We have to find the balance between our faith and our emotions. Do not allow your emotions to dictate your decisions.

Don't allow your decisions to be based on how you feel. Allow your decisions to be based of the Word of God.

The world has a saying, "If it feels good, then it must be right, "but as a Believer, you have to follow the Word.

Even though Jesus' emotions were trying to lead Him away from the cross, He went forward – He did not stop going in the direction God called Him to; and He continued to pray. You have to pray though the situation. How you deal with your emotions will determine whether you experience the blessing or the cursing.

The curse that came on mankind after Adam and Eve sinned was that emotions would try to rule people.

Don't make decisions based on emotions, but on the Word and God.

Don't allow things that look good to the eye to move you.

Factors in making successful decisions vs. emotional decisions are;

1. *Accurate knowledge (Hosea 4:6) My people are destroyed for lack of knowledge: because thou hast rejected knowledge, I will also reject thee, that thou shalt be no priest to me: seeing thou hast forgotten the law of thy God, I will also forget thy children.*
2. *Wisdom and wise counsel*
3. *Understanding the process to reach the desired goals.*
4. *Many problems that people face are based on their emotions.*
5. *Emotions are the source of sin in your life.*
    a. *Once you are born again, you are free from the power of sin.*
    b. *The degree to which you gain control of your emotions is the degree to which you will walk free from the dictates of sin.*

Scripture References

- 3 John 2
- Proverbs 16:32
- Hebrews 4:15
- Mark 14:32
- Hosea 4:6

My desire was to create a book for women by women that would educate, empower, encourage and inspire the everyday women to work on prospering in every area of their lives. I wanted to challenge women globally to make a conscious decision to work on areas that go neglected. Some of us prosper in our finances and neglect our health. Others may prosper in our intellect and neglect our marriage, emotions, or imagination. I believe true prosperity is prospering in every area of your life. The word of God says in *3 John 2 2 Beloved, I wish above all things that thou mayest prosper and be in health, even as thy soul prospereth.* Soul means my mind, will, emotion, intellect and imagination.

I pray that each reader will gain a greater understanding of Gods desire for you to prosper and the will of God for your life will be fulfilled.

In His Service,

Nadia M. Harris

BONUS CHAPTER

❧

Social Media

Social media has taken the nation by storm. Social media is a global platform that is available to anyone and has the ability to reach the world and impact lives globally. Adding this bonus chapter will help to lay the foundation for the upcoming project and give a little insight on how many women are prospering by taking their businesses, gifts, talents and knowledge to the social media platform and profiting by teaching, education, empowering and inspiring others to become Positioned 2 Prosper.

Razor Sharp Social Media Prospecting Skills

Evangelist Chante' Amber Kelly

Social Media Targeted Marketing

Psalms 34:4

I sought the Lord, and he heard me, and delivered me from all of my fears!

In my 18 plus years in network marketing I have heard the cries & the fears of many others in this amazing industry! But the loudest cries and the most disturbing fears have always been; "I don't have the right people or enough people in my network to engage with I believe I'm in the N.F.L. Club No Friends Left LOL!" and or "I don't always know what to say to people when I engage with them or what to say after they have seen my presentation if they have objections!"

Genesis 12:1

Now the Lord had said unto Abraham, get thee out of the country, and from the Kindred, and from the father's house, unto a land that I will shew thee:

My friends you must come out from amongst the old school way of thinking! Long gone are the days of make a list of 100 names including your friends and family, call everybody on the list with a generic script. Invite everyone over to your home, or to a local event pray they show up, the light bulb goes off and they say yes!

Hold on and breathe... The struggle is over there is a better way! And it's called Social Media Targeted Marketing!

In my highly effective, fun and easy to grasp, Social Media Targeted Marketing Mastery class, **(www.socialmediamasterclass.com)** I have taken years of experience with what works and doesn't work, my bachelor's degree in education, and my Super Sonic social media marketing experience and created a course that teaches you how to reach out to a large portion of the 1.64 billion people who are on social media every month! So, you'll never run out of hot leads or worries of what to say!

My Mastery class breaks everything down from point A to point Z giving you razor-sharp skills, professional posture and supreme verbal rap ability to acquire your desired number of customers and or business partners, no matter what your products or services are to create a Massive Passive Income!!!

Here are just a few of the PRICELESS Golden Nuggets dripped in diamonds that I teach you so that you can position yourself 2 prosper and make more money in your businesses!

1. Learn what, how, where, and when to post to get the largest amount of engagements: this will keep you out of social media jail, put you at the top of your friends' feeds, and is one of the many ways I teach you how to get warmed up leads! For example: WHAT to post? You want to post "VALUE" post, "CURIOSITY" post and "HUMOROUS" post. Here is an example of a "VALUE" post; Say you are in the Health & Wellness industry and you sale belly fat burning products, you can do a post of a scholarly article that scientifically shows how "Toxic belly fat can strangle your organs and how to shed it! This gives your audience value on the harmful effects of toxic belly fat and a solution on how to get rid of it! Now. here is an example of a 'CURIOSITY" post say you're in the Credit Repair industry you can wet someone's curiosity whistle by positing a client before and after score with the name of the

client omitted with a 20 sec video attached of them singing your praises and how excited they are that they now have a credit score good enough to move their family into a safer and much nicer neighborhood! WOW! That one will get a tone of engagements I'm telling you! Here is an example of a killer Humorous post (that you can copy the text and then paste it in Google images and they will put in onto a super cool back ground for you for free!) You can say; "Just because a person goes to church that doesn't make them a Christian, no more than standing in a garage makes a person a car" lol!! Oh, Yea baby you WILL get so many engagements. How to Post? You want to post things that relate to your industry mostly. WHERE to post? When posting on Facebook You want to post mostly social things on you personal page i.e. baby pics, vacation pics, milestones, promotions etc... You want to post most business post on your business page because Facebook's powers-that-be like it that way! When posting on LinkedIn you want to post mostly business post because this is a social site that is mostly business people looking to network to increase their revenue streams and you don't want to get booed off the LinkedIn Island!

WHEN to post? You want to post ONLY at peak hours when a large amount of people are on social media to get the best engagement turn-outs!

The peak times are 7 a.m. -8 a.m. (early scrollers)., 12 noon - 2 p.m. (lunch crowd) an 8 p.m. - 10 p.m. (late scrollers & Night stalkers) Note; If you have a lot of friends in a different time zone you might want to add a few extra ones at times they would see your post periodically. Especially if you want to be global! Social media site watch to see how many people engage on your post and that you are reciprocating the engagements! When it's a sweet balance they place you in the top of your friends' feeds! It's a beautiful thing.

2. Learn how to pre-qualify before you even attempt to qualify a prospect: This will save you time & energy! For example; Say you did a curiosity post at between 8 p.m. and 9 p.m. (remember this is one of the peak time frames to post) and your friend Kim responded with a ha ha emoji what you do is before you even attempt to reach out to Kim in a private message to qualify her aka to see if they need something you are offering do this: Go to Kim's profile page and look at her profile picture (does she look approachable is she smiling or laughing or is she looking sad, angry or blanked faced) if she's looking unapproachable most likely she doesn't want to be approached by you, right? Look to see if she is actively engaging on line by the dates of her most recent post. If they haven't been on line for a while then they probably won't respond when you engage

with them, right? Look to see the type of material that she is posting is it upbeat and giving value to others or it is demeaning, arrogant, vulgar or too immature! Look at the BIO is it telling you that she is in your industry i.e. Real Estate, Direct Sales, Health & Wellness etc, is she a mom or wife usually this means they have some family values and want or need quality products and or services! Once she pass the test then she can be written on your list as a warm pre-qualified prospect!! When I teach you this razor-sharp skill and you exercise it is my class and out of my class it will become 2nd nature and you will be able to do this for multiple people and quickly have you a list of warmed up pre-qualified prospects! This skill has been shown to be priceless in it's time saving effects alone!

3. Learn conscious vs. subconscious: this is going to help you know exactly how to break the ice with your warmed-up prospects!

4. Learn the professional way to F.O.R.M. (which means to engage with your prospect about their (F)amily (O)ccupation (R)ecreation and what (M)otivates them) someone so that you are able to inspect to see if they are a good prospect without being suspect lol!

5. Learn how to professionally apply my 3 C's converse, convert, and close!

I will be teaching you MUCH MORE!! All the while I will be giving you PERSONALIZED personal development, tips and tricks AND one-on-one private tutoring aka "REAL-TALK" which is all inclusive with every course level! I honestly believe that you will be blown away by ALL the value you will receive to truly help you explode in your business!!

My friends the word of God is very clear;

Deuteronomy 28:13 kjv: And the Lord shall make be the head, and not to tail;, and thou shall be above only, and thou shall not be beneath,; if that thou hearken until the Commandments of the Lord thy God, which I command thee this day, to observe and to do them:

My master Mentor Dr. Stan Harris aka Dr Breakthrough says; "Procrastination leads to Devastation, it is the assassination of our destination thus we must act NOW!" So the time is NOW for you to learn the razor sharp skills of social media mastery from someone who has mastered it and who has helped many others do the same! Grow your business to the stratosphere and you will position yourself 2 prosper!

Jeremiah 29:11 kjv: For I know the thoughts that I think toward you, says the Lord, thoughts of peace, and not of evil, to give you an unexpected end!

About Evangelist Chante' Amber Kelly

Mrs. Chante' Amber Kelly decided after years of turmoil to live a life of tranquilly, so she gave her life to Christ and started utilizing her Degree in Education with a minor in psychology that she earned partially serving her country in the United States Navy and at Cleveland State University! She is now the Founder/CEO of Agape' Empowerment Service, LLC and specializes in Personal Development Coaching and Social Media Marketing Mastery! She is also a Provers 31 wife to Elder Michael Levell Kelly whom she lovingly calls her BOAZ.

She was given the nick name "The Life-

Healer' by a resident in a drug treatment facility that she shared her story at because of her amazing way she spoke life into the residents that created an atmosphere of healing! She is a stepmom to 2 adorable children ages 12and 16! Mrs. Kelly is a licensed ordained minister of the gospel and walks in the gift of a National Evangelist! And in her own words she says; "She never looks down on ANYONE unless she's picking them up!!

www.socialmediamastryclass.com
anointedsuccess77@gmail.com
216-714-2784

Where powerful people in prominent places pour into your purpose

Linkgenie.net/NadiaHarris